JOURNEYS
WITH
BEETHOVEN

Following the Ninth, and Beyond

KERRY CANDAELE
GREG MITCHELL

~Sinclair Books~

New York, 2013

Dedication: For "the girls" (Danielle, Helena, Camille, and Arielle), and for Barbara Bedway.

Contact the authors at:
kcandaele@gmail.com
Epic1934@aol.com

Twitter: @GregMitch
"Following The Ninth": www.followingtheninth.com

CONTENTS

Kerry Candaele & Greg Mitchell

PREFACE

I am in Vienna, on my last trip for a documentary film I am making about the global impact of Beethoven's Ninth Symphony. I began the journey for *Following The Ninth: In The Footsteps of Beethoven's Final Symphony* over five years ago. Now, having traversed five continents, from China to Chile, from Japan to Great Britain, from Cape Town to Manhattan, I sit in the Café Hawelka near *Der Graben* ("the trench"), a still fashionable promenade where Beethoven enjoyed watching members of the *haute monde* present themselves to their fellow Viennese during the years when he retreated into deafness and isolation.

The day is cold and wet and, for a Californian, somewhat intimidating as I have not, sartorially speaking, anticipated this. Yet I have already made a

morning pilgrimage to the Burggarten, a park near
Vienna's center where Beethoven enjoyed an
occasional stroll. The trees are ablaze in tones of
crimson, the yellow, orange, and red leaves brushed
and pushed by shifting winds and rain in dramatic
counterpoise to the stately Habsburg-era palaces that
serve as the park's border.

I imagine Beethoven meandering through the
park as portrayed by Johann Peter Lyser in his now-
famous sketch, the composer's hands folded behind
him, in black trench coat and top hat, hunched upper
body leaning into life. The year is 1823, it's
November — only six months before the
Kärntnertortheater premiere of what will become the
most heralded symphony in our history. I conjure a
Beethoven to suit my obsession. Oblivious to the
storm around him, Ludwig is hearing the full
blossoming of the third movement of the Ninth, a
music so eerie and serene, so stunningly sad in its
longing in those brief few minutes before the sky is
lit up in the race to the glorious choral climax, the
"Ode to Joy."

It was the third movement of Beethoven's final
symphony that drew me into his world many years
ago when I heard the Ninth, in its entirety, for the
first time. As I drove alone up the central California
coast in the late afternoon light, I found in the *adagio*
and finale a staggering revelation: here was a music
as moving as my beloved rock and soul, as powerful
as the Who's "Baba O'Riley," as tender and touching
as Otis Redding's "These Arms of Mine." I had found
another beautiful reason to feel fully alive.

The third movement seemed to me at the time,
and still today, less a peacefully idyllic retreat than a

yearning "heavenly melancholy," as one early critic had it. Here I found an artist who captured in music the full measure of our predicament as human beings. All of us must ultimately confront the fact that we will remain incomplete, fragmented, often existing in chaotic and inscrutable surroundings, but with a desire for coherence, transcendence even, and constantly on the move toward that inviting and deceptive home that recedes as we approach.

In the Ninth, Beethoven mixes strong accents of despair and disillusionment, even outright terror, and balances these emotions with musical acts of noble and life-affirming artistic creation, and, at times, joy. Within the anguish of his life and music there is Beethoven's *amor fati*, the love of one's fate, and a stoicism that accompanies acceptance. To cite just one example: Playing witness to the cosmic joke that was his increasing deafness, Beethoven wrote in his 1802 *Heiligenstadt Testament*, "Perhaps I shall get better, perhaps not; I am ready." And in the midst of this crisis he wrote to Franz Gerhard Wegeler, "I will seize Fate by the throat; it shall certainly not bend and crush me completely." We have not had many memorable testaments to heroism to equal this—a near-defeated warrior whose spirit is almost spent, and yet remains dedicated to creation instead of destruction.

On that languorous afternoon drive up the California coast, Beethoven had reached me where it hurt. So I started listening—piano sonatas, violin sonatas, cello sonatas, string quartets, concertos, string trios, and the rest—and read biographies by Maynard Solomon and Lewis Lockwood, plus Esteban Buch (on the "politics" of the Ninth),

Beethoven's letters, reminiscences and sketches by friends. I even wandered into the weeds of formalist music criticism, where a musical savage like myself, a man who cannot read the music for "Hey, Jude" much less Mozart's *Jupiter* symphony, should not tread.

As I say, Beethoven got me where it hurt. I had to find out more. And then I had to make a film.

As I studied the Ninth and Beethoven himself, I found that the symphony has had a profound global presence in the nearly 190 years since its first performance, in 1824. For this book I've chosen four examples from my travels.

In Chile the "Ode To Joy" was used by women who sang the "*Himno a la Alegria*" (Hymn to Happiness) in the streets during the Pinochet years, sometimes marching to the walls of torture prisons where those trapped inside heard the music. The Chilean poet and musician Isabel Lipthay took us on a 2,000-mile journey down the coast of Chile to the Island of Chiloe.

At Tiananmen Square in 1989, students played the Ninth over makeshift loudspeakers as the troops came in to crush their democratic moment. Feng Congde, one of the leaders, told me how he and his fellow protestors wanted the world to hear their message of hope for China, and how the Ninth summed up that hope. Congde borrowed car batteries from supporters who lived in the neighborhoods near the square, powered up a pirate radio system and listened as the "Ode to Joy" countered the droning music and speeches of the Chinese Communist Party.

The Ninth in Japan is a rather different affair. Both a lucrative business and a seasonal celebration, the Ninth—known as *Daiku* or the Great Nine—is performed hundreds of times in December, sometimes with 10,000 people in the chorus. Akira Takauchi, a businessman, arranged for me to film a 5,000-performer Ninth at the Ryogoku Kokugikan Sumo Hall in Tokyo.

I met the British folk/punk singer Billy Bragg after hearing that he had written a new English libretto for the fourth movement. He told me how he and Beethoven had serendipitously crossed paths. I wandered with him around the hills and beaches near his home in Dorset, listening as this musical descendent of Woody Guthrie and Pete Seeger found a way to make Frederick Schiller's words live again in a different idiom in a new century. I then followed along as Billy's guest when the London Philharmonic performed the Beethoven/Bragg Ninth, with Her Majesty the Queen in attendance.

During the latter part of filming, in addition, I was lucky enough to travel with Ben and Roz Zander to South Africa, where Ben conducted two concerts with the Cape Town Philharmonic Orchestra to honor Nelson Mandela on his birthday. Ben is not only an accomplished conductor, but he also has the gift of describing in words understandable by a layman what in theory should be indescribable. George Mathew, a Singapore-born, India-raised, U.S.-educated New York City conductor also taught me how to look at the Ninth from multiple perspectives at once, and added his often esoteric descriptions of the music to the film.

In documentary research, I traveled online as

well, having numerous conversations, and a polemical exchange or two, with individuals from across the globe, including my co-author Greg Mitchell, most of them belonging to online classical or Beethoven chat groups. I'm not sure who found who, but Greg (an old friend of an old friend) became a comrade in this Beethoven journey. Unbeknownst to me, Greg—author of a dozen books, former senior editor at the legendary music magazine *Crawdaddy*, and now at *The Nation*—had fallen for Beethoven in a big way around the same time I set out to make *Following The Ninth*. His own journey with Beethoven has been more wide-ranging than mine — that is, well beyond the Ninth — as he studies and listens to everything with the enthusiasm and commitment both of us felt throughout the early years of Dylan and the Beatles.

Greg explores this in Part II of this book, which also includes a brief Beethoven bio and interviews with a pair of leading musicians (plus there's a survey of Beethoven films in the Appendix). And since Greg lives close to New York City, he attends live performances of Beethoven's music at least monthly. After meeting up in New York—before a concert of Beethoven string quartets, of course—and sharing stories about our passion for rock music and "Ludwig van," this book began to take shape.

Many of the most passionate Beethoven fans are ambivalent about a film project such as mine. Some insist that only an exceptional recorded or live version of the Ninth is worthy of their time. Others feel that paying attention to lesser orchestras, choruses, and soloists, as I have, is to neglect the important matter of putting in order, say, the top ten best performances and conductors. And not surprisingly, the divisions that we face in today's society show up among those who have embraced "the Master," as he is referred to often by online aficionados. Many of my interlocutors want a Christian Ninth, and emphasize Beethoven's (always non-denominational) glorification of God or the "almighty," in a libretto or in letters throughout his life.

Others prefer a revolutionary Ninth, as if Beethoven were a premature Marxist. They note that the composer both supported the French Revolution and pushed against the political reactionaries of the Habsburg monarchy, while at the same moment accepting aristocrats' patronage, which created irresolvable psychological tensions, as one of his biographers has argued.

I embrace no singular, uncomplicated Beethoven nor a singular, uncomplicated Ninth. I don't care if he was a virtuous man, did or did not frequent brothels, cheated his publishers, or mocked his colleagues. I despise Hitler's view that the Ninth expressed some kind of Aryan or ultra-nationalist German genius (the Führer had the Ninth performed on his birthday). And I don't believe that the apartheid regime of Ian Smith discovered the deeper meaning of *Alle Menschen Werden Bruder* when it turned the "Ode To Joy" into the Rhodesian national anthem in 1974. ("Rise o Voices of Rhodesia." Sure.) But I hold no brief for Beethoven as political revolutionary. That he believed in human connection across all borders — that the Ninth represents a utopian call to brotherhood, a belief in human progress, and perhaps even a nod to democracy during a time of political reaction—is fine enough for me.

Beethoven had no use for bloated ideologies, strict programs for art or behavior, and no ethical *fatwas* blinded him to the messy reality of life. Beethoven was human, with sins of commission and omission as part of his essential nature. Artistic honesty was his ultimate commitment, music that embodied "a full and unfalsified history of humanity, fantastic yet real, splendid yet terrible," as Austrian novelist Thomas Bernhard described intellectual freedom in his 1986 novel *Extinction*.

I love Beethoven for that artistic honesty, for asserting that the heart and brain that created the world's most profound music was not for sale. His patrons would pay, but Beethoven called the tune. Late in life, Beethoven, even more intently than in the early and mid-period works, insisted on following his own commands, into a musical world of sublime tension and angular catharsis. Especially in his late string quartets and piano sonatas, one hears the fine lineaments of his distress, the quivering hand of a worker in music, tired but not worried by the fact that his strength is leaving him near the end of his days—the "governance of flesh by the spirit" breaking down, as French writer Romain Rolland described the process. I imagine him writing quickly because he knew his life's time has drifted off tempo, *allegro agitato*, then to finale.

As I sit in the Hawelka in Vienna, I imagine Beethoven's hands. Not those of Raphael, a loving display of long and tapered fingers, even in their crenellated age. Beethoven's thick hands were made to scrawl, to be as erratic as his music was to the ears of some of his early critics. His hands were in rebellion against the precious musical world he had inherited, as rude and common as his clothes, impassioned and wild as he scribbled mysterious runes that would be deciphered for centuries to come.

Tomorrow I will film Gustav Klimt's *Beethoven Frieze* (from 1902) at Vienna's Secession museum. The next day, with Isabel Lipthay, the Chilean poet and musician, and our cinematographer, Nick Higgins, I will visit Beethoven's grave. I don't think Ludwig will offer his blessing for the film. Nor do I think he will give me a wink about my endeavor, or pontificate on the best recording of the Ninth to date. I expect to hear nothing from him; for I have already heard everything from him.

– Kerry Candaele

INTRODUCTION TO THE 2013 EDITION

In the year since completing the first edition of this book, I have finished the film that inspired it, *Following The Ninth.* I have been adding here, taking away there, in a fitful attempt to do the impossible: make the film perfect. And yet, as the Japanese know so well because they prize the beauty in imperfection over a sleek lavishness and ornamentation, nothing can be made perfect. And that is a good thing. Or as the poet and songwriter Leonard Cohen wrote, "There's a crack in everything, that's how the light gets in." I do hope the light has got in to this film.

I knew very well when I began that the finished film would never match the one I created in my head and heart. But we must finish our projects if we can. I am pleased that *Following The Ninth* is done, and can now be kicked out of the nest to see how it flies.

I am writing this three weeks in advance of its premiere in Santa Barbara, a beautiful California coastal city that is both friendly to the arts and my home for ten years in the late 1980s and early 1990s. Santa Barbara is also cosmopolitan in its sentiments, a city facing west onto the Pacific Ocean, and perhaps into the Pacific future where China now draws global attention.

And China in the spring of 1989 does play a significant part in the film, where students at Tiananmen broadcast Beethoven's Ninth to the world as they faced down the Communist Party in a brief contest over how the Chinese people would be governed. The film also focuses on other individuals, from Chile to Japan, who crossed paths with the Ninth in the midst of political crises or, in the case of Japan, during a natural catastrophe brought by the earthquake and Tsunami of 2011. Billy Bragg opens and closes the film.

For this second edition, I have added one chapter on Germany during the fall of Berlin Wall where, in the same year as the Tiananmen protest, Leonard Bernstein conducted Beethoven's Ninth in celebration of freedom and unity in a Berlin divided for decades. My coauthor Greg Mitchell also updates his own journeys with Beethoven in the second half of the book.

As the year has gone by, Greg and I have continued to explore Beethoven's music in our own ways. I sometimes focus on the piano sonatas, sometimes the piano concertos, especially the "Emperor" Concerto No. 5, which has the most haunting and beautiful adagio I've heard. One scholar said that Beethoven's music is filled with crocodiles and doves, a way of stating that Beethoven experienced life at such highs and lows and then created musical art that matched his agitation and serenity, his arguments and his musings, and every sensuous space in between.

I am not quite sure if Beethoven the man ever felt at home, except when he made music. I do know for certain that Beethoven has created a musical home for us, filled with comfortable chairs and low burning candles on one side of the room, with shouting tea kettles and brazen klieg lights on the other side. Beethoven, in his many moods and temperaments, allows us to explore him and ourselves with an emotional breath like no other composer or musician. This book and the film are merely small offerings discovered on that musical journey with Beethoven, a journey always in transition, always in flux, and always worth taking.

--Kerry Candaele
May, 2013
Venice, California

PART I

"Following the Ninth"

By Kerry Candaele

CHAPTER ONE

Heavenly Melancholy in Chile

As anyone who knows Chile will tell you, the country is a land of contrasts. From the vast Atacama Desert of the north, to the south where waterfalls, volcanoes and tender and harsh shades of green battle to dominate the landscape that fades into the Zona Austral, Chile is appealingly dialectical: hopeful and melancholy, utopian and hard-headed, a country where poets and artists are considered national treasures. And a country where those same poets and artists were considered, after the military coup in 1973, a threat to society, to be banished, imprisoned, or killed.

My story of Beethoven's Ninth in Chile exists in the middle of these contrasts, a narrative that calls to the melancholy within my own soul, while stimulating the nerve endings of whatever capacity for joy I possess. Like the third movement of the Ninth, in Chile's recent history there is a tranquility interwoven with deep melancholy, a utopian dimension where hope lives; not a blueprint for a good society but as a sentiment and vision for what is possible between human beings.

The Portuguese and Brazilians have a musical tradition, *Fado*, which pays tribute to this complicated emotional blending. *Saudade* is the essence of *Fado*, and captures the Chilean experience of the Ninth for me. The word is not just a way of expressing nostalgia, but rather is a kind of longing and desire to retrieve or recall something lost. *Saudade* understands that bliss is never stable, but always passing, in the same way that one musical phrase moves to another and can only be grasped in fleeting sensations, reconfigured as a whole in memory or another listening.

During my meetings and interviews with several Chileans for *Following The Ninth*, *saudade* was ever-present. The years just prior to the democratic election of socialist Salvador Allende saw the same kind of youth culture emerge in Chile as it did across the globe. In France, Germany, China, the United States, and throughout South America each youth cohort developed its own semi-independent cultural space, with each setting providing a different accent. And decades later, with unrealized dreams and the reality of defeat as constant companions, the Chileans who I interviewed spoke *saudade*, as if the history they had lived was not yet the past, but rather a future to be revived under more charitable circumstances.

In Chile, a new music stole the hearts and minds

of the young intelligentsia. *The Nuevo Cancion* (New Songs movement) pushed slick pop, with its manufactured longing for the girl next door, out of the way. Traditional instruments were revived, ordinary people and their struggles to survive became the subject matter for serious and world-class talents such as Violetta Parra and Victor Jara. Economic classes cross-pollinated, as experimental theater troupes took their wares to the countryside, and it was not unusual to see factory workers at university concerts. The heady mix of left politics and a new culture remains as nostalgia for a lost Utopian moment. Despite the tragedy that would follow the election of Salvador Allende in 1973, everyone I spoke to echoed William Wordsworth's paean to the French Revolution of his own youth: "Bliss was it in that dawn to be alive/But to be young was very heaven!"

Goethe, whom Beethoven elevated above all other German artists, described the terms under which a soul in constant churn amounts to when life itself becomes a work of art: "We must not seek to be anything but to become everything." There is no arrival, no end "product" when it comes to humans who, as Bob Dylan put, are "busy being born" in the act of creation. Romantics like Goethe and Schiller (who provided the text for the "Ode To Joy") did not rely on any outside originator, but instead placed the individual human creator at the center of aesthetic activity. I associate this emotional compound with Chile and the *adagio* of the Ninth Symphony. In my filming from Santiago to Chiloe, I tried to find that music in the frame, a thousand mile journey into an unlikely story about suffering, torture, death, and the capacity for music to sometimes protect or partly heal individuals from harsh assaults on the body and the soul.

I first heard about Beethoven's Ninth and its connection to contemporary Chilean history via an article by Ariel Dorfman. He is the author of many books about literature and history. His play *Death and the Maiden* investigates the physical and psychological terrain of torture and revenge under the dictatorship of Augusto Pinochet, who took power in a military coup, backed and supported by the United States, against the democratically elected Allende on September 11th, 1973.

Dorfman had written about how a version of the "Ode To Joy" called *El Himno de la Alegria* (A Song of Joy) was used in a similar way that "We Shall Overcome" served the civil rights struggles in the United States. The *Himno* was adapted to the Ninth's tune by the Argentine composer Waldo de los Rios, then turned into a world-wide hit in 1970 by the Spanish singer Miguel Rios. Surprising for a pop song in Spanish, the single reached number one in Australia, Canada, Germany, Switzerland, and even reached the "easy listening" chart in the United States.

A YouTube search today for "Ode to Joy" yields thousands of versions, sung by every type of group imaginable, from panpipe orchestras to an absolutely sacrilegious version played on copper bowls. The words in Spanish are a basic appeal to brotherhood and a new day of happiness and peace.

Es cucha hermano la cancion de la alegria

el cantoalegre del que espera un nuevo dia
Ven canta suena cantando vive sonando el
*   nuevo sol*
en que los hombres volveran a ser hermanos
Sien tu camino solo existe la triste za
Yel llanto amargo de la so le dad completa
Ven canta suena cantando vive sonando
*   el nuevoe sol*
en que los hombres volveran a ser hermanos

In the context of a South America dominated by gross forms of inequality between rich and poor, and with several countries ruled by brutal dictatorial regimes, the *Himno* appealed to a basic human desire for a better life, free of violence and the degradation of daily existence under a dictatorship. As resistance movements arose against the military juntas of Argentina, Bolivia, and Chile during the 1970s, the song moved from an intimate and spiritual protest song within the Catholic Church to the streets where the song took on a more aggressive although nonviolent tone.

After the military coup in 1973, the *Himno* was gradually adopted by young dissidents, many of them in women's organizations from all parts of Chilean civil society, who found both solace and purpose in what they considered lyrics of liberation. Often these women would march to the walls of a prison where they knew torture was taking place. They would sing over the walls with the hope that those inside would hear them, an offering, a gift of hope for physical and psychological survival. As cultural expression merged with social movements, as it always does, the *Himno* appeared on the streets of Santiago and other cities as a protest against the torture, against the killing and "disappearing" of those who opposed the regime.

In Chile under Pinochet, the weapons of defense against the arrests, the beatings, the tear gas, torture, and water cannons were, in a minority of cases, the pistol and the rifle. But most often the weapons of resistance from the weak were familiar to those used the world over: bodies marching in unison with others to places of state authority, the banner and the placard, and voices raised in witness for all who cared to see. The *Himno* became a moral force.

And often these citizens in protest against military and police tyranny merely sang. As Dorfman describes the scene, "We sang, over and over, the 'Ode to Joy' from Beethoven's Ninth Symphony, with the hope that a day would come when all men would be brothers." Why were we singing? he asks. "To give ourselves courage, of course."

But why would music, this music, Beethoven's music, composed one hundred and fifty years before, provide courage in a struggle where the means of terror were in the hands of those willing and able to use it? I wanted to find out how the Ninth was a "shield against the suffering and pain" as one of the singers put it, under circumstances that challenge our instinct to live, to flourish, and to love.

Ariel provided names of people to contact, but a few weeks later I still had no clear practical idea of how to follow this Chilean story. I didn't know anyone who could lead me through the streets, introduce me to women who had sung this song of freedom outside the prison walls of Santiago and elsewhere, and, my biggest hope, lead me to someone who had been inside one of these prisons and had heard the music.

I found that person in Isabel Lipthay, a Chilean poet and musician who had been part of the non-violent resistance to the Pinochet regime, but who moved to Germany in 1983, "taking a lot of violence, anger, a bit of the dictator inside me," as she later described the transition.

Isabel is one of the sensitive ones, a member of that strange group of individuals who don't seem to have the capacity, so natural for most of us, to deflect much of the daily suffering that takes place in the world around us. Isabel keeps music, poetry, and playful acts of irreverence around her at all times in order "not to die of the truth," as Nietzsche describes the reason for our embrace of creating. By dropping the veil of protection, she would be driven mad within hours. Like Beethoven, Isabel has a Romantic constitution: not the cliché of a lonely genius tormented by demons while living on gruel in a garret until undone by opium or tuberculosis, but rather like individuals who believe a poem can have power, that creativity is generated from the inside out, expressed in Goethe's *Sorrows of Young Werther* when his protagonist proclaims, "I return into myself, and find a world!"

Her family had immigrated to Chile from Hungary after the Nazis and other Fascist groups across Europe destroyed everything worthy of adulation, including the idea that Western Culture itself could be a beacon to the rest of the world. Isabel took to music, to the stunning nature of southern Chile, and to poetry when her parents separated and she was separated from them both. Pain drove her into art, and she adopted a Romantic temperament, or perhaps it adopted her.

I asked Isabel to be our guide. She would introduce us to her friends, women who had been part of the singers in the streets, and men who had been inside the walls. The bad news (and not really that bad, as it turns out): The two groups of people, the singers and the sung to, lived a thousand miles distant from one another, from Santiago and Valparaiso in central Chile, to the island of Chiloe in the south. So we had to set out for the territories. Our crew — myself, cinematographer Chris Bottoms, Thomas Dinges our sound man, and Isabel — christened our van *Rocinante*, to honor the Quixotic journey around the world to find Beethoven's Ninth. At that point, I still didn't know the global Ninth story. We had to find and shape it as we went.

One of the key differences between feature and documentary film is the question of script. All acted films—except for the ultra avant-garde where improvisation is central to the drama —have scripts. They can and are revised, but basically the shooting runs according to a tighter plan than documentaries. In documentaries, one can have a good idea of how the film will be structured, but the director doesn't set up scenes in the same way as those on a set or sound stage. Improvisation is much more a part of the process.

With Isabel as our guide, we had to visit the people she knew would tell us their story. But we didn't know how they would tell it. On our way south we stopped to interview the poet Clemente Riedemann in Puerto Varas. Clemente was in his mid-fifties when we spoke, with a short greying beard, a child of the South American sixties, drawn to Marxism as an overarching explanation for what ailed his country and continent. He spoke in gentle and eloquent cadences, for once the spontaneously spoken word almost as powerful as the written.

Clemente had been arrested and tortured during the first week after the dictatorship. His father died while Clemente was in prison, "the free gift in a sale on suffering." He spoke in this casual and ironic way about the pain inflicted upon him. "It is the most savage human situation, the humiliation of one's basic humanity," he explained. "Obviously it is worse than death, because when you are dead you do not suffer. You don't know anything. Because torture deprives you of your personal sovereignty in the most extreme way. It's the most extreme situation. It's the most violent, without doubt.

"To be able to survive torture without physical and psychological scars is a very positive thing. Very positive. I think that when I compare myself to other people, I came away mentally rather well. Besides, I was very young, 18, physically very strong, I therefore had a great capacity to resist pain. And psychologically I had a very strong will. I remember I had a hood on and my hands were tied, I said to myself, this will pass, it will be hard, terrible, but then in a few years I will remember this and will talk about it calmly. That is what I was thinking in that moment, even before I suffered the harshest sessions of torture. I had this certainty, as if my mind crossed the abyss of torture, and I did not see myself dying there. I saw myself crossing it with difficulty, but I saw myself on the other side."

I sat astonished while listening to Clemente's story. Many in Chile cracked under similar circumstances. He had been instructed by his political organization on what to expect and how to endure torture, but hearing him talk calmly several years after the fact about the worst kind of suffering put me off guard.

Conducting these kinds of interviews is difficult. When individuals address painful psychological trauma in front of a camera, I have an instinct to draw back, as if to try and protect the person from his own memory, simultaneously protecting me. Over the years of making films, I've learned to merely sit and listen, to see where the story goes without directing. I put my list of questions to the side, and wait. In interviews like this, I don't need my questions answered, and I certainly don't need to interrupt with a question that will take the discussion some place else, according to "the plan."

Clemente also reminded me that Chile's *Himno* was always reserved for significant moments. It's not a song that was sung all the time, or without good reason. The song was always connected to massive events of great importance, moments requiring great concentration and emotion, when people needed a lot of hope.

The *Himno* showed up in the religious liturgy of the Catholic Church, was sung at funerals, and even after important athletic victories, in situations when the community came together. Clemente said "this hymn has the ability to communicate what everyone feels. This song is like a seal of consecration of something sublime, it's beyond the everyday, something to be aspired to, united in the same emotion, the same idea of the continuity of life."

But what would I do with Clemente's words when it came time to edit the film? A film full of "talking heads" would be tedious, no matter how insightful or moving the testimony. Because, in the Ninth Symphony, Beethoven takes us on a music journey across the landscape of human emotions — terror, serenity, sadness, exuberance and joy — in every country I visited I wanted to capture both the beauty and the ugliness of the human and natural landscape. The Ninth embraces all. The music and choral text examine the darker strains within our human drama, and folds them into the very story of human redemption and joy of the fourth moment. I'm reminded of a contemporary song by Bruce Springsteen that captures the soul-healing and capacious embrace of Beethoven's Ninth. It's called "Land Of Hope And Dreams":

> *This train carries saints and sinners*
> *This train carries losers and winners*
> *This train carries whores and gamblers*
> *This train carries lost souls …*
> *This train carries fools and kings*
> *This train, all aboard*

The Ninth carries everyone, top to bottom and across the globe, and therefore the film was designed to replicate the symphony itself. Clemente's recounting of torture would serve as "voice over," a darker part of the Ninth, perhaps with abstract images from the B-roll (shots of non-essential characters and footage of the countryside) to push the story along in an unorthodox way. I think Beethoven would approve.

We drove south from Puerto Varas to the jump off point for the Island of Chiloe. Our merry band and *Rocinante* had a day to wander before we had to meet our next interviewee, a man who had been in prison ten times, had been tortured by the security police, and had heard the Ninth sung over those prison walls to political prisoners.

Stopping now and then, we filmed a stunning multi-colored valley at odd angles through barbed wire, or to let the cows and sheep cross in front of us. Driving on dirt and gravel roads provided a meditative atmosphere to what the camera would "see," making longer-held shots almost imperative. We could turn left or right onto smaller roads. It didn't matter, as long as we could find our way back and on to our interview at the planned hour of arrival.

As the day was getting on we came to a crossroads. After a bit of discussion we decided to go left, for no other reason than "just because." Ten minutes later we arrived in a small village with a couple hundred years of boat-building history to walk through. We had about forty minutes of "magic hour" available for shooting: the time when the sun sits low on the horizon, the light gets warmer and soft, and the shadows lengthen. We were just having fun, mind you, just wandering with no idea what we would find.

What we did find was both lyrical — in that sense where all the right words come together without effort, where emotional harmony seems to prevail above all else — and lucky. We parked near an old church in the center square, and as we got out of *Rocinante* we heard music. Hmmm, ok, as following the music seems to be the theme of the whole enterprise, we followed the music. We arrived at a house where a band inside was playing traditional *Cueca* music, Chiloean style. Should we knock, invite ourselves in, ask if we can film, risk being considered rude and aggressive? Easy answer. Yes. When making films, one must take chances.

Not surprisingly, given the general friendliness of Chileans, the musicians (two women and three men) invited us in, welcomed the cameras, and proceeded to play a batch of traditional songs they would perform at a celebration in the town square the next day. Isabel joined in by playing one of the many drums scattered about the floor.

After a few songs, and feeling a bit more comfortable, we then asked the obvious question: "Do you know the *Himno*, the song based on the Ninth?" They laughed in unison. "Of course, who doesn't know the *Himno*?" And off they went, with Isabel singing, into a version of the "Ode To Joy," Chilote-inflected. I stood there thinking: We turned left instead of right, and we found this incredible meeting of the hearts and minds. No script needed. Just serendipity.

When going on adventures such as this, a trip across the globe looking for a good story to tell, one can never know whose voice, eyes, way of telling a personal tale will resonate long after the interview is over. On the Chilean trip, that voice, those eyes, that story belongs to Renato "Machi" Alvarado Vidal.

Our caravan circled back from Chiloe to visit Machi in the city of Puerto Montt, a region called Los Lagos where two volcanoes Osorno and Calbuco sit in watch over this "capital" of Chilean Patagonia a thousand kilometers south of Santiago. A week later in Santiago we would meet a group of women who stood in front of prison walls where they knew that on the other side men were being tortured. Today, interviewing Machi, we heard the story of a man who heard those women and believed, for only moments at a time, that those voices would keep him alive.

But more than his words, the look in Machi's eyes tells his tale. His eyes are mischievous, challenging, diabolical and unflinching when he declaims against his political enemies in the Pinochet camp, or in self-mockery when he describes his personal ideology as "the people, rock and roll, and marijuana." And before he was robbed of his pacifism, Machi was a self-proclaimed "anarcho-psychedelico," a party of one and one million at the same moment.

After the coup in 1973, he joined one of the many Marxist groups in Chile. Almost everyone in the opposition did the same. I was engaged by how he told his tale, smiling and chuckling at both right and wrong moments — say, in the middle of describing a torture session, or how he tossed vile insults at his tormentors so they would beat him instead of asking him questions about his colleagues and comrades.

Most who suffer torture do not survive intact; more are drowned, in some form or another, than are saved. How do those who survive make it? As Primo Levi, a survivor of Auschwitz, remembered without gloss or romance, some will harm another prisoner in order to live, others will give up on life in order not to suffer further indignities. And many who do survive will suffer shame and guilt for willing themselves to live outside the camp or the cell.

On being innovative under extreme duress, Machi and his comrades had to use the delight in smelling bad to lift the spirits, as strange as it sounds. He and three other men were forced into a small box, standing upright against one another for days at a time. Machi took inspiration and perspiration and, like the wily alchemist that he is, suggested a stinking contest to pass the time. The one who came out of the box the most malodorous would be the winner. What did the winner win, what did they all win together? Merely joyous sanity, creating laughter together inside a prison from which many did not return, and a chance to begin again one more day.

Others, outside the walls, were innovative, too. Women of conscience and courage came in large numbers to sing the "Ode To Joy" to those inside. Machi heard them. He heard them sing "stink it up again my friend, go on stinking and living until we get you out and wash your body clean." He heard them sing "we will drink wine together again *companero*, sluiced from the fruit of the land that you love with all your heart."

Chris Bottoms, our main cinematographer, filmed many other scenes in Chile — in Valparaiso, Santiago, and in small towns along the central highway that runs north-south through the country. We met "witches" who knew the *Himno* and sang it at 3 a.m.

in the middle of a prison yard. A Cuban trumpeter trained in the classical tradition played the Ninth for us on a Valparaiso street simply because we asked. We filmed a young couple dancing the traditional Chilean *cueca* on the rocks near a beach at sunset, moving in silhouette as we circled around them with cameras and sound equipment, and a guitarist and stranger nearby recruited for the scene. This scene is now dispersed throughout the film—just one more episode not in the script, but inspired by the music and images of beauty all of us carried amongst our equipment.

Follow the music. I wrote out this simple but demanding phrase on the first page of my notebook for the film. There were plenty of other ideas for the project, derived from philosophical, cinematic, or personal sources, but following the Ninth's music seemed the best mantra and priority for the film. But the nagging question of how to actually translate this capacious, complex, and often unwieldy symphonic music into another medium dogged the proceedings. Whenever I felt lost, or that the journey was out of focus for whatever reason, Isabel put me back to the course. Having left Chile for Munster, Germany in 1983, she is a poet in exile, after all, with the capacity to present a complex world of emotion in a few notes: "Love was sick under the dictatorship, because we couldn't trust anybody we didn't know. So we had to be silent for the person we loved. I think love is difficult everywhere, all the time, because it's much work. But under dictatorship, love is more difficult than usual. And yet love and music were the only places we could find tenderness, and friendship, too."

But the Ninth was like a shield for Isabel and many others, a balm for the suffering and hurt, and even a source of strength to continue, sometimes in hard struggle against injustice, sometimes for connecting to another person without the necessity of complex speech. The Ninth, like Isabel, expresses an optimism that transports us beyond reasoned analysis. How on earth can people embrace joy and brotherhood during times when there those feelings are so little in evidence?

The simple answer, as if the impulse were written into our genetic markers, or literally given hand-to-hand across the terrain of culture, is that we must. And it is a weighty act to make joy and brotherhood a choice. Beethoven made that choice. Sick, completely deaf, confronting his own mortality, having suffered deep pain and misery in his often desperate search for love and family, Beethoven chose hope, not just for himself, but for all humankind, as what can fairly be called his last will and testament. Beethoven, with Isabel, Clemente, Machi and millions of others, chose the Ninth.

CHAPTER TWO

Billy Bragg Meets the Queen

Every generation finds its own new version of the Ninth. But who would have imagined that the British folk/punk singer Billy Bragg would provide a Ninth for our time? As Billy describes his strengths and limitations, a Beethoven Billy Bragg Ninth (I now call it BBB9 for the sake of efficiency), at first glance seems not the most likely marquee billing for the classical set.

"Not being a great guitar player or not having a great voice, what I did have was, I felt a great ability to articulate my perspective," Billy once explained, "a perspective that I didn't see reflected anywhere else in music, so I guess it was that sense that this was a voice that should be heard. And the way that I saw the world was something that drove me to try and get out there and communicate..... Maybe I should have been one of those nutcase guys who stands on an upside-down milk crate on the corner of the street shouting to people, but actually I ended up being a singer-songwriter."

For anyone who has seen Billy play, the self-description is fine as far as it goes, leaving out only just how charismatic this one-man-band with a sole electric guitar can be. Having imbibed The Clash and other bands from London's punk's 1977 *annus mirabilis*, Billy distills the social vision of Woody Guthrie, Pete Seeger, and early Bob Dylan and combines it with the kinetic spirit of Joe Strummer on a very good night.

Bragg doesn't play songs, he tears through them like heat lightning, as if thinking that this night might be the last, that this one song might end it all with a pulse that had flat-lined, and wanting the final thing he did to be the best thing he did.

Thankfully his sets are not all fourth movement rock rousers. Ramones concerts felt like that — they didn't do *adagio*. But Billy has also written some of the more tender love songs that have come out of England in the past twenty years. It's like having Joe Hill and Sam Cooke in the same band. And unlike Dylan on stage, Billy loves to talk, to joke, to preach political sermonettes, to remind his audience that here stands a human being, not a cynical brand. His wickedly funny between-song-jives are alone worth the price of the ticket. His audiences are not at a gig but in fact *in* on it. The busker in him never died, a sly recognition that he just might one day be back on the platform at the Charing Cross Station or that every concert is the Charing Cross Station. A Billy Bragg show always brings the circle of friends closer, tighter, as if after two hours it might just remain unbroken for the rest of a dreary week. He's famous for hanging out after the gig to sign shirts, provide photo ops and to just chat.

He is unpolished and unposhed, a working-class bloke from Barking who is as unapologetic about his democratic socialism as he is about his love for Marmite. That's yeast extract to you, mate, just magnificent he claims on almost everything eatable and never to be confused with the Australian counterfeit. Billy doesn't leave home without it, and does a lot of needless explaining at airport security lines.

So how did it come to this, Beethoven and Bragg on the same ticket? And as Billy put it, "what am I going to do if Beethoven finds out?" Asked in 2009 by the Southbank Centre to write a new libretto for the Ninth in English, and risking the wrath of the purists, Billy responded with typical élan, true to the sentiments of Schiller's and Beethoven's words but revamped for a new century. It was, in a way, the reverse of his famous and very successful *Mermaid Avenue* project in putting some of Woody Guthrie unpublished lyrics to music.

Others (most notably the artist, activist, and polymath, Paul Robeson) had sung various English versions of the "Ode To Joy," but none had, as Billy put it American style, "taken it all the way into the ninth inning," by not just translating the words but rewriting them. When I heard through the internet grapevine that Billy, whose music I had collected since his debut, had tackled the Ninth, I was stunned. First, here was a guy who came out of the punk tradition and he had rewritten *the Ninth*. Second, how strange and timely, and thus meant to be.

Now, one of the things that many non-filmmakers don't realize is that getting in touch with famous people is not easy, and in fact is almost impossible given the number of people who stand guard around them, massaging egos, fetching coffee, or negotiating deals. I wrote to his website, explained my project in brief and received a call from Billy himself within hours. This ain't no *Entourage*. That's punk, the do-it-yourself ethos in action.

Billy and his wife Juliet and son Jack had just stood in the backdraft of a Ninth concert performed for the first time with a version of his words, and sung by 1500 choristers from across England. He was still floating above ground from the experience when we spoke. As Billy described the event later, "you can look at the Mona Lisa, but you can't really embody the painting, any painting. With the Ninth it's different, you can embody the music by recreating it, by singing it." I knew I had to film a BBB9, and soon enough I was on a plane to London and then down to the Bragg home in Dorset on the south coast of England.

We walked and filmed the hills and beaches just outside his door, where Billy spent time walking his dog and jotting ideas for the finalized lyric he was assigned to complete in five days. And why not, he asked, "I'm a songwriter," a signal that in his mind the distinctions between so-called high and low culture had little meaning when tackling Beethoven's most popular and populist work. Billy knew the Ninth, and had heard it performed live. He picked up the Leonard Bernstein 1989 "Ode To Freedom" version performed after the fall of the Berlin Wall in

1989 and proceeded to torture Juliet and Jack by becoming a human jukebox, incessantly reworking his new words in the shower and out.

After touring his old neighborhood of Barking, a suburb of London, and visiting his high school where Billy gave a talk about Rock Against Racism (the movement that transformed his life and showed him the power of music to change lives and make political history), we sat for several hours in various places and brought Ludwig van and Billy Bragg into focus.

I asked Billy about his personal career path: "There must have been points at which you felt like 'this is too difficult' or 'I'm not going to make it.' Or did you have a sense of 'This is my destiny' and you were going to achieve it?"

"No, it's more like, 'There's gotta be another way of doing this.' You know, when you're presented with the idea of rock music involves two guitars, bass and drums and big amplification and spandex trousers, you find....you seek out another way to get that power and immediacy, and for me it was playing solo with an electric guitar. That was something that allowed me to confront my own demons about being afraid of getting in front of an audience and making a fool of myself. But also to sort of ram home my message, you know, that pure lyrical content backed up with electric guitar didn't inhibit in any way what I was trying to put across. Whether they were love songs or political songs.

"There was no great eureka moment when I suddenly realized this was my destiny. It was more like plotting to escape from a destiny that had been planned for me by the people who lived in a town where there was a car factory. I was educated to work in a car factory. If I wasn't going to work in a car factory I had to have a real good plot to escape...almost escape from a prison camp. So, playing guitar and writing songs...I wasn't very good at boxing, I couldn't play football. That seemed to me to be the most viable way of avoiding having to work for the motor company.

"And I'm certainly still to this day driven by an urge to communicate. I think it was something that I had in a sort of very general way up until I was about 19 years old and then punk rock happened and I kind of super-charged it. I made it into more than just a dream, I made it into a cause. And I've tried to serve that cause ever since."

Two days later I heard the BBB9 live for the first time. The London Philharmonic performed the Beethoven Bragg Ninth, with Her Majesty the Queen in attendance.

Billy's mum, even after 25 years still unsure about his line of work, let him know that she now viewed his career choice as honorable. She stood with pride and watched her son shake the hand of Queen Elizabeth II. Billy responded to the occasion with an arresting article for the Daily Mail two days later: *How The Queen Charmed the Pants Off Me.*

I could see that Billy Bragg charmed the Queen as well. I sat about twenty feet from the Royal Box. I couldn't tell if she was tapping her foot, and she certainly was not rattling her jewelry in time. But I did notice Queen Elizabeth digging into the new libretto, her eyeglasses held steady with one hand as she read Billy's English words to the tune of the

"Ode":

> *What's to be then, O my brother?*
> *Sister, what is in your heart?*
> *Tell me now the hopes you harbour*
> *What's the task, and where to start?*
> *Though now speak ten million voices*
> *Every word is understood:*
> *Furnish every heart with joy and*
> *Banish all hatred for good!*

The Queen looked up from her program and nodded in the direction of the chorus. The world, it seemed for a moment, had turned upside down.

Later, Billy reflected on the evening: "Well the performance was something special because obviously, you know, the Queen's at your gig, that doesn't very often happen to me. So that in itself was a bit of a treat, and also I got to invite my mom, which was quite important, you know, for mom and the Queen to be in the same room at the same time to hear a piece of music that bought me a lot of brownie points at home. I mean it was a strange. I mean just out of pure curiosity to have a chance to look the Queen in the eye, it was too good to miss.

"I'm sure she does this all the time, but she came up to me and she gave me this look that sort of said, 'So what the bloody hell are you doing here Braggy? What is all of this? Beethoven, Queen, what are you doing here?' And I sort of began to explain a little bit about the process and how I became the person who wrote this new libretto, and finished off by saying to her, 'I set out to become the new Bob Dylan and I ended up being the new Frederick Schiller.' And she said, 'Oh, that's nice.'

"And then we all laughed and that was it. The Queen left and it was all over and everyone relaxed and went upstairs for drinkipoos, and then I got a phone call from one of her footmen, 'Would it be possible for her majesty to have a copy of the score signed by Mr. Bragg?' I mean, it's wacky. Let me be honest, lots of people hang around after the show to shake my hand and get an autograph, but that, that takes the biscuit."

Near the end of an interview after the concert I asked Billy a question that most people I spoke to for *Following The Ninth* find odd or out of the blue, as it is my concern and not, until I ask, theirs. The question is about despair and the melancholy that I find in parts of the Ninth, even in the finale where everyone rises to sing a song of brotherhood and joy. For the joy will come to an end with *our* end, we will be all be rendered null, and nothing will remain. A sense of ending, even joyous endings, demands that we consider the journey we are on at the moment, perhaps with the end in sight providing an opportunity to render the present in brighter hues. Or so goes the ideal during late evening reveries. Beethoven was gravely ill when he composed the Ninth, a man with a knowledge of his own mortality, and the accumulated sorrows and the "mischancing of human affairs," as William Faulkner described his life and art.

Billy, ever the optimist, responded in a way that I thought he would. "The fourth movement certainly within the Ninth Symphony is the victory of humanity over despair. That's what the chorus is doing at the end, that's what they portray, this high water mark of joy and victory. This is the victory snatched from the jaws of defeat. This is humanity ultimately asserting itself over despair, over cynicism. That's the joy that Schiller celebrated. That's the joy that Beethoven saw as far as I'm concerned.

"Yeah, I think if you're involved in the creative process you're busy giving birth to stuff all the time. Birth to ideas, birth to performances, birth to the creative spring: If it flows it constantly refreshes. Sure yeah, one day it will.....well actually it won't. One day we won't be here any more, but the spring will still run. People will still be able to hear our songs and sing them.

"You know, Beethoven's well does not run dry. He's no longer here and we're still capable of being moved to ecstasy by his creations. So Beethoven wins, the worms lose."

CHAPTER THREE

Feng Congde and Tiananmen Square

In China today the vast majority of young people do not know anything about the events at Tiananmen Square in the spring of 1989. Despite pronouncements to the contrary, the pervasiveness of the internet does not mean that history cannot be wiped away by the Chinese Communist Party (CCP) if the need requires. And, naturally, with tyranny comes the need to constantly clean up the past, to silence voices of resistance that echo from Tiananmen to Tahrir and back.

Many, perhaps most, people in China today are not interested in the iconic "Tank Man," or the movement for liberty and freedom, begun by students but eventually attracting a cross-section of Chinese society, crushed in a instant when the threat to the state reached fever pitch. At the risk of generalization, most Chinese people are busy riding the tiger of economic development that rivals any country in the world. But history provides its surprises, as Egypt teaches once again. A Tiananmen in Tahrir may one day lead, in some inexplicable way, to a Tahrir in Tiananmen II.

Twenty years after the People's Liberation Army (PLA) crushed the student rebellion at Tiananmen Square during the night of June 4th, 1989, I sat with Feng Congde, one of the student activists honored with a ranking as one of the "Top Twenty-One Most Wanted" in the days and weeks after the massacre near Tiananmen. He is a humble and gentle man, and deeply reflective about the tragic events. After the crackdown, Feng Congde hid out in the Chinese countryside for months, then left the country for Europe and finally landed in the United States. Today Feng works to cure "erased history syndrome" with a human rights NGO near San Francisco.

When we met in a hotel room in mid-town Manhattan, I heard somewhat shocking testimony about the people who occupied the square during those historic months, and much more.

On first reaching out to him about appearing in the film, I said I didn't want to revisit the complicated and well-reviewed events on the Square, but rather to talk specifically about how the Ninth Symphony was a part of the big story, and his personal story. I wanted to know what on earth made Feng embrace a bit, and then a lot, the abstract ideas of democracy, freedom, and the fact that lowly students could attract attention not just from the Chinese government but from the whole world? Feng didn't want revolution; he wanted to feel alive.

He wanted to feel that life was not just grunt work, not just capitulation to the absurd idea that we were put on earth to continuously obey frozen platitudes, the ascent to "success," or to kowtow to a corrupt patriarch and his party.

Thankfully, he agreed to talk about everything I was curious to know. After discussing basic facts and how the Ninth was taken up by the students on the Square as an anthem of hope, Feng told me that rather than thinking that the protest against the government was a political movement, he insisted "it became a collective artist movement, when each student, each citizen, became naturally an artist of hope….for us and for China."

Months later, after looking at the interview several times, and after watching seventy hours of ABC and NBC archival footage, I was still baffled by the comment. How could one of the main leaders of the student outrage (which later turned into a protest by millions of Chinese from every sector of society), have come to the conclusion that 1989 was not a political movement?

The government certainly understood the protests as political, a direct threat to the Chinese Communist Party monopoly of power across the board. And just as certainly, the students had a list of political demands, including freedom of expression, freedom of the press, reforms to the educational system, the end to corruption, and a host of other concerns that struck directly at the Communist Party power to order the daily lives of Chinese citizens. So what did the students, those who went to the Square in the initial days, understand about what they were doing? What did they understand about themselves, what they were put on this earth to accomplish?

Feng had certainly lost hope in his country, while most of his peers wanted nothing more than to buy whatever they could get their hands on, to wait it out for the main chance to become part of the growing upper middle class in China. If they were lucky, savvy, connected and corrupt, these children of the turn-to-capitalism after Mao's death could get rich off the very peasants and workers designated as the *sine qua non* of world history by Communist Party ideology. And yet wealth and status often do not draw everyone into their charmed circle. An individual temperament, a few books one reads during college, an important teacher or colleague whose life and values look attractive, can encourage one to try to make history rather than just making a "living."

I understand Feng's sentiments in the context of similar social movements led by students in the United States during the 1960s, and now with Occupy Wall Street. Middle-class security was no substitute for the sense of recognition and nobility that comes with standing in solidarity with others who also felt that the road to success, as defined in terms of a successful career and social "respectability," was a bad deal, emptiness squared, a glittering con. Not surprisingly, acting with others for a common purpose led not to the mentality of the herd, but to a strengthened sense of one's own personality.

Being inside the crucible of a social movement can bring out the desire to be free in the broadest sense of the word, in body and in mind. But how does one change a country? In Feng's case, he went to Tiananmen Square because…his computer broke down.

Without a working computer to further his imagined career, he took a walk – actually an unknowing leap — and went to observe the protests. Such decisions are strange, innocent and contingent, mocking our self-aggrandizing idea that we can know exactly what we are doing in this life and where our road leads. As the wise saying goes, Man thinks, God laughs. Or as John Lennon put it, "life is what happens to you while you're busy making other plans."

Feng was busy making other plans and life called out to him: "engage with your time, young man." Two months later he was wanted for "crimes against the state" by one of the more repressive governments on earth. But that story is not quite right. It's too linear. That story lacks mystery; it does not, and cannot, tell us anything about the inner man.

The more time I spent with Feng's words, the closer I moved to understanding what he meant. In part, my feeling for who Feng was as a singular human being helped the process, and watching the footage again and again pushed me closer to sympathy with Feng's "artists of hope" sensibilities.

Before joining the students on the Square, Feng did not see himself as a political person. He, like so many young Chinese intellectuals, wanted to leave China—"we were so disappointed in this country, we had no future"—feeling that the country suppressed what was most valuable in a human being, the sense that life could be a creative process of becoming who one really is. Presenting the problem in such a way, with the Nietzschean admonition to "become who you are," may seem abstract, nothing to get upset about. Listening closely to Feng's words added bulk to the bone.

It was obvious that Feng didn't want what most of us are taught to want. Before the student movement began, Feng had received a scholarship to pursue a Ph.d at Boston University. He had been studying English, taking the required tests for admission, and thinking about a dream job in a foreign country: "Like the young students now in China, we cared just about ourselves, wanting a better job in western Europe or the United States, and we cared nothing for society. We just wanted to leave." And then his computer broke down. Twice.

Feng became a reluctant leader. But the comic often rides in tandem with the tragic. Had Feng's computer not broken down at precisely the moment when students were taking Tiananmen Square as their own, he might now be with a hedge fund in Manhattan. But it did break. And taking a risk that would seem utterly foolish by those standing on the outside looking at his life and future prospects, Feng went down to the Square to eventually arrive at a better understanding of who he was as a human being.

Six weeks later Feng discovered that he was willing to die to improve the Chinese nation. He became, in some important sense, who he always was. Once on the Square, Feng found not just a movement of political liberation, but an inner liberation that was perhaps more important for him over the long term. Feng described the events on the Square as a "festival of the oppressed," words borrowed from Lenin to describe the early stages of the revolutionary process.

Watching those many hours of footage in the NBC and ABC archives in New York provided a better sense than words just why this sensitive man chose Lenin's phrase as a metaphor for what he experienced. Similar to the euphoria of Tahrir Square in Cairo, the early days of the protest were all celebration, as if for the first time in their lives these young men and women felt what it was like to be truly alive to the possibilities of a life well-lived in deep connection with others.

Hierarchies of leadership and vigorous differences in tactics and strategy among the student demonstrators developed over time, with errors of judgment and their real political consequences to follow. But in the early days, life on the Square was a utopian moment, not of blueprints for a better society. Common cause in intimate interaction came in every manner.

Documentary film-making is a tricky business. History is contested terrain, to be fought over and often shaped by partisan commitments. When the participants in the actual events are still living, and the historical moment under scrutiny is as monumental as the protests at Tiananmen Square, the battle over historical truth is likely to be fierce. Scores will be settled, hot emotions sluiced into every line of the narrative. And if television video footage becomes central to transmitting the story, the problems mount.

George Black and Robin Munro captured the problem well in their book *Black Hands of Beijing: Lives in Defiance in China's Democracy Movement.* "At the best of times, the medium [television news] has a wretched relationship to historical truth, saturating its audience with powerful, instantaneous images that are not easily revised," they wrote. "But television, paradoxically, is never more powerful than when the screen goes blank." Black and Munro argue that news teams near Tiananmen Square got the "massacre" completely wrong, a fact confirmed by subsequent research. There were very few students killed at Tiananmen, with the vast majority of deaths occurring in the streets and neighborhoods leading to the Square. Students would be hunted down after the final assault, imprisoned and tortured, with some, like Feng, escaping into exile.

The working class of Beijing suffered the massive physical violence, which demonstrates a key fact about the uprising: Tiananmen was not merely a student movement, but rather a people's movement that involved millions throughout China who sympathized with the students' demands — an unnerving reality for a government that monotonously reminded the population that it alone represented the best interests of the peasants and proletariat of China. Like the newspaper man, who burns his notes after seeing what happened in the final gunfight in John Ford's *The Man Who Shot Liberty Valence* says, "This is the West, sir. When the legend becomes fact, print the legend." Western reporters fell in love with the legend, and the Chinese government has printed next to nothing about the Tiananmen events, preferring to let historical amnesia eliminate the conflict altogether.

A full story of the Tiananmen events in film was told

in the 1995 documentary *The Gate of Heavenly Peace*, which is both comprehensive and complex in its attempt to tell the "whole" story. My intentions were of a different type altogether. I was interested in how Beethoven's Ninth crossed paths with Feng and his comrades on the Square, and what this music meant to Feng and others, and what role it played in the symbolic battle, the battle of voices that was played out during the six weeks of the uprising.

As the students had no weapons, music and other forms of symbolic communication would serve as a fragile carapace under which students and others could shape, if only momentarily, the resources for resistance while simultaneously telling the world via music what their struggle meant. Or as Feng put it, "We used the Ninth to create an ambience of solidarity and hope, for ourselves, and for the people of China."

And true to every social movement, the students spoke in various accents. Freedom banners appeared everywhere, often written in English with a sense that the whole world was indeed watching. Clever hands built scurrilous effigies, witty epigrams competed with scatological humor for space on cardboard signs, and later, during the final days of the protest, the iconic "Goddess of Democracy" was carried to the center of the action. The *papier-mache* and foam statue, sculpted by students from the Central Academy of Fine Arts, was large and menacing to those watching from Party redoubts, as it resembled the Statue of Liberty. A tent city was built, and a minor infrastructure cobbled together for handling the everyday problems of food distribution and keeping conditions sanitary (again, echoed years later at the many Occupy Wall Street camps). And the marching, the shouting, the trucks and buses with people on top arriving from throughout the city and countryside just didn't stop. And then there was the music.

One image in the footage that appears again and again in the early days and weeks of the protest: people singing. The communal joy is obvious, impulses given free reign, righteous ecstasy coming out from its hiding places into a nearly soulless situation for students in China who wanted more than the dreary future on offer. Singing commanded attention and brought people face-to-face with what Feng called "their dignity as human beings," as if for the first time.

Beethoven's Ninth provided a bridge for those connections. Classical music in general and Beethoven's Ninth specifically was considered a symbol of Western bourgeois decadence and cultural imperialism by the Communist Party, especially during the years of Mao's "Great Proletarian Cultural Revolution" from 1966 through 1976. Even in 1989 Feng felt the lingering effects of a decade when the "violence of culture" meant "all the good things were denied. If you liked modern dance, that was bourgeois. If you liked modern painting, that was bourgeois."

As a member of the intelligentsia, the embrace of "counter-revolutionary" ideas — and who could tell what these were from day-to-day — made Feng a suspect in a thought crime yet to be committed.

On the Square, Beethoven's Ninth became part of Feng's crime against the state. Once engaged as an organizer, Feng set up a makeshift broadcasting system, cobbled together with car batteries and loudspeakers provided by both university students and working people from the surrounding neighborhood. The improvised system could not compete with the government speakers that lined the Square, broadcasting the droning speeches of Lin Peng and other lesser apparatchiks who tried to convince those arriving by the tens of thousands to stay home or return to school.

Feng described a singular moment on the Square when Beethoven's Ninth summed up everything he hoped for his country.

With over a thousand students on a hunger strike in the Square, Li Peng announced martial law on May 19th. The droning began in earnest: "Comrades, in accordance with a decision made by the Standing Committee of the CPC Central Committee, the party Central Committee and the State Council…to restore normal order in society, and to maintain stability and unity in order to ensure the triumphant implementation of our reform and open policy and the program of socialist modernization….Their [the students] goal is precisely to organizationally subvert the CPC leadership….The reason that we were so tolerant was out of our loving care for the masses of youths and students. We regard them as our own children and the future of China. We do not want to hurt good people, particularly not the young students." And on and on, with the carefully chosen audience clapping on cue.

In the Square, Feng pulled out a cassette. "The students, when we heard the announcements," he told me, "we were so angry — and I put on the cassette of Beethoven's Ninth to cover the voice of the government system. So there was a real battle for *voice*. Hundreds of thousands of students shouting, as we broadcast the music on the square louder than the government system. I just had a feeling of winning. Of triumph."

Feng played the final movement of the Ninth, featuring the "Ode To Joy" with the key line *Alle Menschen warden Bruder* ("All men will be brothers) because "it gave us a sense of hope, solidarity, for a new and better future. And it was really fantastic that it changed us, transformed us. We feel finally we regained our dignity as human beings. We were separated by the government, but now we are free. We just feel free. So on the square, we feel a collective feeling of joy. We were free at last."

The Ninth is high-wire music written without a net below. Once in a while disparate experiences, different artifacts a long distance from one another in time and space, come together and make perfect sense. Beethoven's Ninth Symphony at Tiananmen Square squawking over small speakers as the troops were coming to crush the movement makes perfect sense.

But the fourth and final movement at Tiananmen did not end in a transcendent shout of joy: "We just feel a real new hope — and the tanks and the machine guns killed that hope." I will never forget the look of utter despair on Feng's face when he said those words, the memory of defeat, a movement of hope put down hard and bloody, captured by the camera.

Still, remind myself that the person sitting in front of me in that New York hotel room spoke of

Tiananmen as an artists' movement and a search for the source of life, his ultimate commitments. Although Feng's talk of "artists of hope" and the rest could be taken as naïve, I think that he is using metaphorical speech, the metaphor of poetic memory, manufactured by a "part of the brain," as the novelist Milan Kundera describes the process, "that records all the times when our hearts have been touched by all that is sublime, all that is beauty."

For Feng, the days spent making history on China's most famous public space were sublime and beautiful. To be sure, the Tiananmen events are for many of the participants now illuminated by the aura of nostalgia, a small vice perhaps, if one is willing to allow that defeat often goes underground, only to emerge in victory in a different form, often unrecognizable, and a surprise to those who have stopped paying attention to the past as it lives in the present.

A more generous interpretation of Feng's specific memory, the slippage from the art of politics to politics as art, is offered, appropriately, with his own words: "We wanted to express ourselves, we wanted to find the hope, find the sunshine, to find the source of life." At a time when we as a people seem tired of hope, when the word hope itself seems a tired cliché from a world far away, the artist of hope still seems a worthy occupation. It's an appropriate moniker for someone making a film about that which is rich and everlasting in both the revolt of Tiananmen Square and in Beethoven's Ninth Symphony.

CHAPTER FOUR

5000 "Daiku" Voices in Japan

The Ninth (*Daiku*) Symphony phenomenon—and I choose that word with care—in Japan is one of the more unusual adoptions of any cultural artifact on the face of the earth. And following the Ninth in Japan with a camera is both delightful and burdensome, which is why I returned three times to make sure I got what I needed for my film.

On one side of the ledger: Japan might be the only country where one can book a karaoke room and choose the "Ode to Joy" as a song to ruin with drink-soaked cohorts, in German. Like most experiments in spontaneous collective vocalizing in a pub, it sounded good at the time, but when the recording was played back in the silence of an editing room, I found that what I had captured resembles police sirens and a nearby dog pound. I loved the experience of cacophony in a country known for its subdued indirectness in all things except when cheering — no, screaming — on their beloved baseball teams.

Because the burdensome side of the ledger is that, in general, the Japanese are a reticent people. Getting a Japanese man or woman to talk about personal matters takes some doing. And in documentaries, it's personal matters that matter.

But not entirely. *Following The Ninth* is an ensemble piece, where several protagonists come and go, a sharing of the stage in keeping the story alive. The more clever documentarians will find one protagonist to carry the arc of the film. Even better, if that person is quirky or notorious and famous — think Hunter S. Thompson — the epicenter is obvious. Or, in ensemble films, if there is a contest involved, then the story arc is quite simple: You follow the trails of four or five contestants — in (pick your competition) a spelling bee, a Scrabble tournament, a ballet dance-off — and the film writes itself. It ends when the winner is announced and catharsis reigns.

In *Following The Ninth*, I have a dead genius, several living protagonists, a massive piece of art stretching to about seventy-five minutes (depending on the tempo) in four movements, ten countries to visit, commentators to corral, all of which had to be organized into a ninety-minute film. That spelled trouble. If I could get a couple of these people to bare their souls for the camera — Beethoven had already done so in the music — the drama would help the film. But I knew I would not find any baring of souls in Japan.

What I did find, however, was equally important. Every December the Japanese perform Beethoven's

Ninth hundreds of times, from north to south, from schoolroom choirs to the best professional orchestras in the country, and often with five or ten thousand people singing the "Ode To Joy." The Ninth in Japan is grand, and mysterious in many ways, where Beethoven stands as a national hero fitted to the Japanese psyche (if I can be pardoned for the generalization), and the symphony itself turned into a second national anthem.

Beethoven-as-hero in Japan means that he embodies many things that Japanese, with the young perhaps the exception, hold dear. Certain key words and traditions, with a long legacy in Japanese culture, are critical for understanding the Ninth's continuing relevance for Japan. *Kando* (to be emotionally moved/touched), *akogare* (longing for or dreaming of a sought after goal), *gambaru* (to strive for and work hard to achieve the difficult goal), and *moriagaru* (to spark one's life), are examples of feelings that Japanese take with them to the singing of the Ninth, ways to maintain a tradition of endurance and perseverance in day-to-day life. (Thanks to *Daiku* scholar Eddy Chang for these insights).

Common nonsense about "Samurai spirit" does not apply, even though fierce nationalists, who combined a martial and even imperial urge within recent Japanese history, used these notions to horrible ends in the middle of the last century. In today's Japan, Schiller's text and Beethoven's music are now firmly attached to notions of peace and international camaraderie, with the long admiration for German culture in general as a distant afterthought. Group effort in achieving individual goals, or in overcoming personal hardships, is now at the center of the *Daiku* experience.

And often enough the desire to sing with thousands of others is merely an act of pleasure seeking. As one seventy-four year old woman put it, "I always wanted to sing the 'Ode To Joy' on stage. That's why I joined." Yutaka Tomizawa, a choir director, says, "The members all have different experiences. Some have been singing for a long time. Some have never sung before. But the purpose of the choir is not performing on the stage. It's to stimulate their lives in their twilight years." Singing in German is difficult enough, and memorizing the piece even more so, but as Tomizawa points out, "there's nothing like the Ninth. It seems impossible for amateurs to sing, but Beethoven casts a spell on you. Many start off thinking, 'I can't do this,' but then other members urge them to try harder, and working together they get it done. The feeling of accomplishment is sublime."

My challenge as a filmmaker was to capture this grand experience and present it in a personal and complex fashion, capturing the nuance and wonder of the Ninth in Japan at equal turns.

Once I thought I had a certain advantage in the pursuit. I used to teach Japanese history and culture at a private boarding school (Cate) near Santa Barbara. So why did I feel so befuddled about the country and its culture when I arrived and traveled thousands of miles in search of the Japan Ninth? Some who have traveled to Japan feel as if they have finally found "home," and stay on in a country that is, on the surface, like many developed nations, except without the grime, crime, chaos, and trains that don't run on time.

The answer is not a simple one, as I am still somewhat off balance in reflecting on my travels, and how my understanding of one of the most beautiful countries in the world has changed since this project began.

As a quick sidebar, my more leisurely travel to other countries through the years has been less satisfying except when on the job. You know, the kind of travel where "we did Germany, Italy, and France," then return home with the photos. I am not saying that such travel (that tends to be not as leisurely as we expect) is not worthy of our time. I note merely my own increasing discomfort with the visiting of the usual sites, without the opportunity to live a bit amongst those who know where to find the best noodle shop in Shinjuku.

I feel the same way about world-class museums. I don't want to walk for three miles in the Louvre with thousands of others, catching a glimpse of three hundred pieces of art about which I know little. I prefer to sit in front of one painting or one artist, having studied a bit prior to the confrontation, perhaps discovering the mysteries revealed by the brush strokes and the odd perspective on that squirrel in the bottom left corner of the frame, or to decide that one of these treasures should be thrown out the front door on its ear.

As everyone who does business in Japan knows, one cannot travel to Japan empty headed. To prepare yourself with a study of Japanese customs and history is a big plus if a major *faux pas* is to be avoided. And since I wanted the entire crew (three people) to know something of how to think and feel about our surroundings while filming, I requested that the cinematographers read two books about Japanese aesthetics, and to revisit a couple of classic Kurosawa films along with a bit of contemporary Japanese cinema, to be viewed on our little screens on our long flight. What better way to see the past that lives in the present as we went about our business? Or so I thought.

The first book, written by the American, Donald Richie, who has spent his adult life studying Japan, is *A Tractate On Japanese Aesthetics*. In seventy-two pages Richie introduces the reader to Japanese beauty, "in the manner of a *zuihitsu*," ideas that "follow the brush wherever it leads." And the brush leads us to fascinating insights: about elegance, the simplicity "in the precise stroke of the inked brush, the perfect judo throw, the rightness of the placing of a single flower" — emphasizing the concept underneath rather than the surface "realism" of much western art. Japanese aesthetics is "revealed as the product of a social competitiveness, of the desire to find yet more subtle shades of meaning and beauty than the next guy."

As beauty in Japan comes in small packages, the second book was Junichiro Tanizaki's exquisite *In Praise of Shadows*. Tanizaki's observations are lovingly presented in forty-two pages, where he covers toilet practices (much has changed since he wrote the book in 1933), Buddhist temple architecture, and thatch-roofed houses, among many other things. But unlike Richie, Tanozaki's reflections are enlivening but mournful, as if he was trying to preserve a passing Japan in the act of writing. He

directs the eyes, with a steady and practiced hand—
an expert in the calligraphy of the five senses—to the
little things we miss, in Japan and by implication
elsewhere, when we won't or can't slow down long
enough to see, hear, taste, smell and feel what
surrounds us.

Tanizaki writes, "Japanese music is above all a
music of reticence, of atmosphere. When recorded, or
amplified by a loudspeaker, the greater part of its
charm is lost. In conversation, too, we prefer the soft
voice, the understatement. Most important of all are
the pauses. Yet the phonograph and radio render
these moments of silence utterly lifeless. And so we
distort the arts themselves to curry favor for them
with the machines."

And again, "We do not dislike everything that
shines, but we do prefer a pensive luster to a shallow
brilliance, a murky light that, whether in a stone or
an artifact, bespeaks a sheen of antiquity." Who
cannot sympathize with such thoughts, which
remind me of T.S. Elliot's response to his first visit to
Times Square: "It might be considered beautiful,
provided one didn't know how to read." Japan now
has many Times Squares, with their full commercial
neon assault on the senses.

So there was much to learn. About how to see
with different eyes, about how to present a business
card, how low to bow when meeting a respected
person, about how and when to present a gift so as to
not embarrass the receiver. And still the major *faux
pas* was always one minute or one step away.

One instance will suffice. I visited a small
restaurant in Kyoto with my wonderful guide to all
things *Daiku*, Akira Takauchi, where I stepped on a

tatami mat with my shoes on before sitting down to dinner. A collective gasp came from those Japanese who witnessed the transgression. But in general, the Japanese forgive visitors their violation of decorum, the thousands of rules for behavior developed over centuries and now written into the DNA of Japanese life, decorum now being quickly discarded by a good slice of the younger set. Once considered shameful, a young woman who puts on makeup in the subway is now common. Positive change, in large and small ways, has been accepted in what is a fairly conservative society.

One small, and false, victory came my way during an important lunch with administrators for what's known as the *5000 Daiku* in Tokyo. I was asking permission to film their concert. After two hours of eating, talking, and considerable silence — the Japanese, unlike Americans, are not uncomfortable with silence during conversations — Akira told me I was "very Japanese" because I listened attentively instead of talking. Not hard to do when I know only ten words of Japanese. I had to pick up the hefty check. But I was given permission to film. No complaining allowed.

In comparative terms, Americans are anarchists, always looking for that imaginary space where no laws or rules apply, setting out for new territory whenever we get the itch for change. We have no aesthetic tradition that coheres or guides art over the long haul, but rather a mélange of individual urges and desires that have emerged out of the rough-elbowed jostling of immigrant-filled cities, with change and innovation as the only sure mantra that inspires worship. We have our painters in the genre of rural nostalgia, just as we have novelists who write westerns, but they don't rate.

The Japanese, by contrast, are not anarchists, metaphorically speaking, although beneath the surface calm and orderliness of Japanese life there is a hot magma that surfaces in *anime* and the grotesqueries of some *manga* comics. Modernity has its way with everyone, eventually.

In one of my final interviews for *Following The Ninth*, a large door was opened for me onto Japanese culture. My interviewee told me that one of the worst insults a Japanese person could say to another is a three word phrase that roughly translates as "you are oblivious to the atmosphere in the room," which means you are either rude or ignorant and definitely selfish about how to engage others in a society that prides politeness, where how one treats others is based on a precise and refined knowledge about where one stands in relation to specific individuals. There is a hierarchy of long standing, and attention to it must be paid.

After all the reading and teaching, it turned out that it was I, the educator, who needed educating. There I was with my dunce cap in the corner of the Japanese culture schoolroom. But as strange as it may sound, I enjoyed being ignorant. I was constantly picking up cues about Japanese life, discovering, in the inimitable words of our former Secretary of Defense, Donald Rumsfeld, the "known unknowns" about Japanese culture.

As the team traveled throughout Japan, we filmed stunning Buddhist temples hidden in the mountains three hours outside of Tokyo, taking time to bathe in one of the many glorious bath houses that are the envy of any hot tub-loving sensualist who thinks that Esalen of Big Sur fame is the best one can do in this life. We visited an elementary school where young men and woman were practicing the "Ode" for a local performance, and watched a rehearsal—one of hundreds in every major city—where amateur singers practice with a *sensei* for six months, trying to wrap their tongues around the dastardly German language so as not to embarrass themselves as they stand next to strangers and friends and sing out.

I traveled to Naruto in Tokashima Prefecture, to the site of the first Ninth performance at a concentration camp for Germans during World War I. German prisoners made their own instruments, taught the Ninth to Japanese outside the camp who then played to the assembled inmates what must have been one of the most ragged versions of Beethoven's final symphony. The German House museum near the original camp holds some of the original instruments, and presents, in word, diorama, and artifact, what has to be one of the more friendly concentration camp experiences the world has seen. Is this an overly strenuous attempt to reassure visitors that World War II Japan is the anomaly and not to be scrutinized deeply or in public displays of national self-flagellation. And it is here, where the past is either reconstructed for therapeutic use, or when the cultural practices of present make amends for sins committed by forbearers, that the Ninth plays a part.

For not only is the *Daiku* a winter phenomenon that provides a decent income for conductors who go from town to town putting local musicians through their paces, but it is also a peaceful and welcoming Japanese face presented to the world. And since it is no secret to anyone that Japan has been, and prefers to remain, an ethnically and culturally homogeneous society, "all men will be brothers" provides a rhetorical lift to the spirit, even while the quotas for all those brothers wanting to immigrate to Japan remain quite strict. And yet I am convinced that the use of the Ninth in Japan—and the Ninth has been used and abused almost everywhere since the day it was born—has much more to do with the bright side of Japanese life than the dark.

I filmed three concerts in Japan, and each one seemed more a chance to celebrate life than any conscious attempt to do international diplomacy by other means. And each concert displayed varying atmospherics and tone, with the inevitable differences in how the piece was conducted, but also in the purpose of each rendering.

In every instance, however, filming a concert, with one's eye behind a lens while searching for the right framing—anticipating the burst of a clarinet solo, the roar of the timpani, or the passion embodied by the conductor's hands as he (sadly, there were no women conductors there) presses the chorus to a crescendo, and making sure to capture the action on time—challenges the eye and diminishes the ear. Like texting while driving, something has to give, and it's often the front fender. Sadly then, filming a concert makes it difficult to listen to the music with the required attention to find the nuance of soundscapes and emotional content within the rhythm and tempo of each movement.

The challenge of listening while filming was especially acute on my second trip to Japan, where I filmed a concert with 5000 singers at the Ryogoku Kokugikan Sumo Hall in Tokyo. As anyone who understands the physics of sound will tell you, singing in unison with 5000 people, most of whom are a hundred yards away, is like trying to have a clear conversation using two tin cans and string. And if the person standing next to you was slack in his German lessons and turns *Alle Menschen* into what sounds like Swahili, the troubles can magnify as the musical payoff tanks.

But somehow it works. It works because the vast majority of Japanese who participate take their Ninth as an ultimate commitment. Joy may be the theme of the "Ode," but pride in the accomplishment is the singer's motivator. Besides, the *Daiku* experience in Japan is as much, if not more, a social ritual as a musical one. Everyone, participants and audience alike, is assured that the Vienna Philharmonic in no way will be challenged by these concerts. Certainly no one in the Vienna Boys Choir carries photos of a recently deceased relative in his pocket, or holds a written reminder of what is to be accomplished in the new year when taking the stage, as many Japanese do. The Ninth in Japan vibrates to a unique set of internal commands than anywhere else on earth. And thank goodness for that.

For the third and final trip, I was fortunate enough to travel with a small group of Japanese-American men and women who belong to the Los Angeles *Daiku* Singers, who sang in a benefit performance for victims of the earthquake and tsunami. Tragedy crosses paths with joy and reverence for a life that is transient, subject to both beautiful and horrifying surprises. But the Japanese, especially those with a connection to vanishing traditions under assault by all things modern, understand transience and the inevitability of all that is beautiful being lost to time's lovely and corroding embrace.

We, as visitors, may think the cherry blossom has its perfect promise of life as art when in full bloom, while the Japanese, inheritors of a long history of an aesthetic of imperfection and decay, see the fading of the bloom as the more exact and exacting correlative to life, and equal to radiant abundance. And they are right to think so. As the last chord of the Ninth begins to fade, the singers look to those standing near them and understand fully that some of their friends and countrymen will not be there to sing the following year, that within the joy of the Ninth there is also nostalgia for a longed-for utopia that is improbable but not yet impossible.

Beethoven did not give us a utopia-as-blueprint for a good society, with seating charts nicely arranged and platitudinous moral chapbooks for all. Beethoven did, however, offer in the Ninth—strange as it seems from a man with such a socially isolated sensibility and sense of himself as superior to most of his fellow mortals—an iconoclastic rhetoric of emancipation and self-fashioning, on a large scale. Beethoven's "kiss for all the world" embodied in Schiller's "Ode To Joy" indeed seems grandiose, above his station, if one merely considers Ludwig's class position within aristocratic Vienna. He certainly carried his class resentments on his sleeve. "What you are," he wrote to Prince Lichnowsky, an erstwhile benefactor, "you are by accident of birth; what I am, I am by myself. There are and will be a thousand princes; there is only one Beethoven. " Of course Beethoven need not have worried, for his inner resources, imposing talent, and his powers of emotional alchemy that transformed bile and love and joy and sorrow into musical gold, were always at his call, placing everyone, justifiably, at his service.

So was Beethoven creating a small utopian lodestar with the Ninth, setting all things right with his conflicted inner world, and hoping against hope that all of us, if only at irregular intervals, are capable of solidarity, connection, identification, and a care and concern for others that knows no boundaries?

We will not know exactly what Beethoven was thinking when he composed the Ninth, for the record of his comments on the piece is thin. Yet I am convinced that present in the Ninth, especially in the heavenly third movement, is a Paradise lost as well as one gained. There is a realization that a moment of bliss has passed, and as the philosopher Simon Critchley suggests, "happiness is never distant from the experience of melancholy….happiness recalled is more intense than happiness experienced" because it is accompanied by a sense of a journey on its way to the end, and like our meditation on a stunning sunset, we know there are only so many of these moments left to us on this earth. A tragic optimism is at work here, the affirmation of life's beauty and vitality while understanding that suffering is ever-present and unavoidable, and it is Beethoven's artistic and personal triumph. It is a sensibility that the Japanese who sing in the *Daiku* seem to embrace.

The choir director Tomizawa agrees. "I think it's because of their age that the members of Choir become so deeply involved in the Ninth. Some are survivors of the Tokyo air raids, so the notion of peace expressed by the lyric, 'Be embraced, you millions,' affects them in a very personal way. That's why they sing so movingly, because it comes directly from their hearts. They aren't just memorizing the words."

I have become jealous of those who stand as equals and sing the "Ode." Having seen close to fifty Ninth concerts, I have yet to sing in one. I would like to, preferably in Japan—if the L.A. Daiku would train me up.

CHAPTER FIVE

Berlin and an 'Ode' to Freedom

In December, 1989, Lene Ford lived and worked in East Berlin just blocks from the Berlin Wall. Lene, twenty-one at the time, was not very political, and grew up taking the division between East and West Berlin for granted, a fact of life imposed upon the German people for, in her somewhat vague but accurate formulation, "political reasons."

Indeed, Lene was not alive for one of the key flashpoints between the United States and the Soviet Union during the Cold War, when in August of 1961 tanks sat on either side of Check Point Charlie in Berlin facing each other as the new president, John F. Kennedy, and Soviet Premier Nikita Khrushchev played a dangerous game of chess that could have provoked nuclear war. On August 13, Khrushchev settled the question by erecting a barrier around East Berlin, first with barbed wire, soon followed by an eleven-foot concrete wall.

Politicians in Western Europe and the United States expressed outrage, but in private Kennedy and the others felt that the Berlin Wall at least was better than war. For twenty-eight years the Wall would keep an unstable and repressive German Democratic Republic (GDR) in place, until the events of 1989 brought it, and East German communism, down with surprising speed and little violence.

Lene Ford was more surprised than most. For her, the GDR was not just a country she was brought up to love, and to which allegiance was owed. Lene enjoyed being a child there. Shortages of consumer goods were real, the arrest and detention of every manner of dissident was appalling, and the state control of civil society, from sports leagues, to cultural organizations and labor unions, was almost total. But Communist (Socialist Unity Party, or SED) education propaganda held that they were creating new kinds of humans, with egalitarian values and virtues. Like most people, in whatever country, she didn't make it her business to challenge state power, dictatorial or democratic, focusing on day-to-day life rather than making history by protesting, resisting, or raising her voice in opposition to violations of human decency.

When Lene was young, and her family stayed clear of any trouble with the Stasi (the pervasive GDR secret police), she believed the claims that the west was an imperialist monolith, bent on destroying the Soviet Union and the communist experiment. Western television was for Lene the "television of the enemy," dangling its bourgeois delights in front of the citizens of the GDR in order to undermine their patriotism and sap their socialist will. No surprise, then, that Lene cooperated with institutions designed to secure her loyalty. Lene was a member of the state-sanctioned and controlled Thalmann Young Pioneers and the Free German Youth (*Freie Deutsche Jungend,* or FDJ), created by Soviet and GDR authorities to co-opt and channel youth in a politically safe direction.

A young person might play football or chess with other FDJ members, or sing in a chorus, but "Marxist-Leninist-Stalinist" ideology was the guiding force in all activities. German artistic heroes were recruited for the cause, as FDJ members paraded through the darkened streets of Weimar with fire torches in 1949 in honor of Goethe. Bach Year had followed in 1950, with an FDJ-sponsored Beethoven Year in 1952. And since both Goethe and Beethoven were considered by SED ideologists to have been "working toward [Marxist] dialectical materialism, without realizing it," Lene crossed paths with Beethoven early and often. As she described the encounter: "I remember being taught the Ninth Symphony. And what I always dreaded was we had to sing the 'Ode To Joy.' And we got graded on it, and everyone had to do it."

Lene still keeps well-protected photographs of her receiving the highly desired red scarf awarded for service to the socialist state when she was ten years old. "I was very, very proud," she says, "and gave a lot of support, and help, and love to my country...back then." Millions of people in the GDR lived what can be called normal lives, as long as they did not stray far outside SED lines. Those lines were easy to cross. Moral transgressions were political transgressions, such as sporting long hair or listening to subversive rock music from the west. But as Mary Fulbrook points out in her social history of the GDR (*The People's State: East German Society from Hitler to Honecker*), most of the time "the FDJ was totally incapable of dominating the lives of most young people."

And like most children, when she got older, Lene's imagination began to wander and stray, as she "dreamed of going over to West Berlin, to meet all these people we secretly watched on T.V....I could not grasp the Wall in its entirety," she said "but I knew there was something else behind there, and I wanted to go there one day." Lene's relationship to the Wall consisted of both fear and longing. On occasion she feared being shot by the men who stood in the watchtowers that overlooked the "no man's land" between East and West Berlin; at other times her desire to see the rest of the world opened up into fantasies about a Western dream-scape, less dreary, less confined than the life she knew.

Lene took to writing pen pals as a hobby, corresponding with people from several countries, including teenagers from the United States. But "they were fiction to me" she says, "I was never going to meet them. There was the Wall." The Wall, for Lene, was both symbol and real, a sharp line between a story that could only be written in epistolary form via imaginative leaps into a world where people moved in wider circles of experience.

And because she imagined, and wrote, across barriers and received letters in response, a close friend of the family began to check on her for the

Stasi, a shock and a deep hurt, for she loved this "uncle" who betrayed her for reasons that remain obscure: "Probably they [the Stasi] thought I was political, that I want to run away, or set something up." She had unintentionally attracted political heat, the inevitable results followed: "You can tell a child something, for ten years, for fifteen years, but then there will come the day, what all children do when they grow up, they start asking questions."

Several thousand miles away, a man who could have been Lene's grandfather had been asking impertinent questions for most of his life. Leonard Bernstein, the renowned musician, conductor, educator, political activist and composer, would join Lene near the Brandenburg Gate in the winter of 1989 as the Berlin Wall was cracked open and thousands of East Germans poured through to be united with their German brothers and sisters after twenty-eight years of separation.

When the Wall started to come down in November of 1989, Leonard Bernstein was seventy-one years old, and in failing health. In ten months he would die of cancer. "Lenny," as he was called by those who knew him, was a precocious musical polymath, a magnetic and enthusiastic advocate for the belief that music could transform lives and in the process transform the world.

A talented pianist, Bernstein composed both high and low--symphonic pieces for the world's best orchestras, and Broadway musicals for the masses (*West Side Story* being his most lasting commercial success). After talking over as the music director for the New York Philharmonic in 1958, Bernstein became America's first conductor/celebrity, presenting popular Young People's Concerts for CBS throughout the late fifties and sixties, and lecturing widely. He spoke to his growing audience as Lenny, not the distant maestro of the European tradition, and conveyed both profound understanding of the complex works of Beethoven and Mahler and other composers within the classical canon, while at the same moment translating music into words that non-musicians could understand. Bernstein loved the spotlight, and television provided a bigger stage on which to perform.

Bernstein insisted that composing "was like a religious experience," a "trance state" where, if successful, the composer conceives a "totality, a Gestalt...that is going to work, upside down and backward." Even when conducting he was composing on the podium: "If I don't feel I'm Beethoven, I'm not doing it well."

His identification with Beethoven was long lasting, and more than just musical. Bernstein's social activism began in his youth, and was consistent throughout his life. His support for organized labor and the civil rights movement, including his notorious (in mainstream media circles, at least) 1970 fundraiser for members of the Black Panthers, and his protests against the Vietnam War earned him an FBI tail and a place on the U.S. State Department blacklist for a time. Leonard Bernstein at one point was put on a list of people to be moved to an internment camp in case of a national political crises.

Tom Wolfe labeled Lenny's political commitments "radical chic," but Bernstein didn't play at politics, as his New Deal idealism existed both before and after his rise to celebrity. In the final decade of his life, he campaigned for nuclear disarmament, for AIDS research funding, for the abolition of world poverty, and for the utopian impulse articulated in Beethoven's Ninth Symphony, that one day "All Men Will Be Brothers" (*Alle Menschen werden Bruder*).

Bernstein had described his feelings about the Ninth years earlier in one of his television broadcasts that were a hit on American television during the 1950s (he also devoted an entire program to dissecting the Fifth Symphony, with musicians arrayed across part of the score painted on the floor). Bernstein associated the words of love, peace, brotherhood, and joy to the year of his birth, 1918, when an armistice brought the World War I to an end. He added the folk song phrase "ain't gonna study war no more" to the key words that he associated with Beethoven's Ninth. "We are all children of one father," he added, "let us embrace one another, the millions of us."

The Ninth, he rightly insisted, "rang[es] from the mysterious, to the radiant, to the devout, to the ecstatic," but the words of joy and peace are hollow and ineffective when, as Bernstein described the reality of our lives, "we have not yet found ways, short of murder, to act out our suppressed rages, hostilities, xenophobias, provincialisms, mistrust and need for superiority. We still need some kind of lower class as slaves, prisoners, enemies, scapegoats." This impulse embedded in the Ninth, in Bernstein's words, is not a blueprint for a good society. The "crooked timber of humanity" cannot be made straight right here and now. To desire perfection in human beings is to desire the impossible.

But Beethoven, Bernstein believed, represented "struggle, struggle for peace, for fulfillment of spirit, for serenity and triumphal joy. He achieved it in his music, not only in his triumphal Ninth, but in all his symphonies. And in his quartets, his piano sonatas, and trios and concertos. Somehow it must be possible to learn from his music by hearing it. No, not hearing it, but listening to it, with all our power of attention and concentration. Then, perhaps, we can grow into something worthy of being called the human race."

Leonard Bernstein brought his history and his sentiments, if not his youthful exuberance, to Germany for two performance of Beethoven's Ninth in December of 1989.

The first concert was timed to end at midnight on December 23, when the border dividing the two Berlins would be fully opened for the first time in twenty-eight years. Then Bernstein conducted the Ninth at East Berlin's Schauspielhaus on Christmas morning. While more than a thousand gathered in the hall, hundreds more stood in the square in front to watch the performance on a giant television monitor. On the live TV broadcast, Bernstein declared, "I am experiencing a historical moment, incomparable with others in my long, long life." By then more than 200,000 East Berliners had visited the West for the first time, and about the same number had traveled East. The Associated Press reported, "One West Berliner riding a bicycle and dressed as

Santa Claus failed to persuade border guards to let him through ahead of the rest of the crowd."

In keeping with the Ninth's theme of connection across borders, the orchestra included members from the Dresden Statteskapelle and the Bavarian Radio Symphony Orchestra, as well as from orchestras from the four countries that technically still occupied Berlin--the New York Philharmonic, the London Symphony Orchestra, the Orchestre de Paris, and the Orchestra of the Kirov Theater, Leningrad. The chorus was made up of singers from both sides of Germany.

Bernstein wrote a friend about the concerts: "I'll be reworking Friedrich's Schiller's text of the 'Ode To Joy' and substituting the word *Freiheit* (Freedom) for *Freude* (Joy). Because when the chorus sings *Alle Menschen werden Bruder*, it will make more sense with *Freiheit*, won't it?"

In the filmed performance of the Christmas concert, one can see Bernstein conducting more with his facial expressions more than his hands and arms, what one observer called an "eyebrows only" directing of the musicians. His cheeks puff out, his eyes dart, he stands erect but weakened by age and illness, but still shaping the music by what Israeli conductor Itay Talgam called "doing without doing." Bernstein described this democratic "late style" as how the "conductor must not only make his orchestra play, he must make them want to play. He must exalt them. Lift them. Start their adrenaline pouring. It is not so much imposing his will on them like a dictator. It is more like projecting his feelings around them...It doesn't really matter how well you move with your hands. It should be in your face, it should be in your expression."

Bernstein received as much pleasure in conducting the Ninth that day as he gave. Sherry Sylvar, an oboist who played in the concert, said, "When the chorus sang the word *Freiheit*....I shall always remember how his face lit up."

In fact, a good part of the world lit up. The concert was broadcast live to more than twenty countries, to over one hundred million people, with a recording released on in 1990 as the *Ode To Freedom: Bernstein in Berlin*.

The famed conductor had added playful humor to the occasion by imagining that he could make a career of performing the Ninth around the world: "I can't wait to do it in North Korea and China." But he always came back to his first principles when it came to Beethoven. "The dubious cliché about music as the universal language, almost comes true with Beethoven. No composer who has ever lived speaks so directly to so many people, the young and old, educated and ignorant, amateur, professional, sophisticated, naive, and to all these people, of all classes, nationalities, and racial backgrounds, this music speaks a universality of thought, of human brotherhood, freedom, and love...

"In this Ninth Symphony, in the finale, the music goes far beyond the [Schiller's] poem, it gives far greater dimension and vital energy and artistic sparks to these quaint old lines of Schiller. This music succeeds, even with those people for whom organized religion fails. Because it displays a spirit of Godhead and sublimity in the freest and least doctrinaire way. It has a purity and directness of communication that never becomes banal. It's accessible without being ordinary. This is the magic that no amount of talk can explain."

And if there was one person who could explain Beethoven's music in words that all can understand and embrace, it was Leonard Bernstein. He speculated that "perhaps there was in Beethoven the man, a child inside that never grew up, that to the end of his life remained a creature of grace, innocence and trust, even in his moments of greatest despair. And that innocent spirit speaks to us of hope and future and immortality. And it's for that reason that we love his music now, more than ever before. In this time of world agony, we love his music and we need it. As despairing as we may be, we cannot listen to this Ninth Symphony without emerging from it changed, enriched, encouraged. And to the man who could give to the world so precious a gift as this, no honor could be too great, and no celebration joyful enough. It's almost like celebrating the birthday of music itself."

After such a verbal performance, along with Leonard Bernstein's life and music, one can only stand and shout, Bravo, Maestro, Bravo.

When Lene Ford made her first journey outside of East Berlin, the experience, she reflects today, was the pitch-perfect emotional moment in her life.

She recalls the walk to freedom: "The distance to me seemed endless. And for the first time in my life I had an understanding of how big, how far that no man's land was. I got there and people started touching me, handing me tissues. And they all said welcome, and we love you, and they hugged me and

I didn't even know these people. They were cheering on us. When I got there it was like a parade. There was just pure love and joy. I wish every person on this planet could experience this moment. It just fills you from head to toe, an"

Lene felt, on that day, what most people feel when they are lucky enough to find the better parts of themselves in those rare moments when people find their way to a common humanity beyond the egotism and selfishness that life often demands. Two decades later, reflecting on the meaning of the fourth movement of Beethoven's final Symphony from her current home in Los Angeles, she recalls her feelings as she walked through the broken Wall into a different world and a new life: "The 'Ode To Joy' for me means that all human beings are equal. No one is less, no one is more, no one is better, no one is worse."

That day, The Ninth as school catechism and doctrinal instruction had, in an instant, been transformed into an open hymn to a just order, a physical and emotional space where for a moment all might stand face-to-face as members of the human race, nothing more and nothing less.

PART II

"And Beyond"

By Greg Mitchell

CHAPTER SIX

Roll Over, Chuck Berry

What was I doing, at eleven in the morning of my 60th birthday, at Avery Fisher Hall in New York for the first time since a Springsteen concert more than thirty years earlier, waiting for a French pianist and Swiss conductor to play a piece of music that recently meant nothing to me at all? Why was I suddenly breaking out in tears on the subway listening to some haunting instrumental music not even on my radar or iPod a few days before? Why was I now practicing my Italian (*cavatina, adagio, fortissimo*) when I had refused to do that even before visiting Venice? How is it that in a space of a few weeks the rock 'n roll I had loved, and written about, for decades – from The Kinks to Arcade Fire — was supplanted in my iTunes library by a long-dead composer, as this evolved from a new passion to a mighty obsession?

Why was I now debating, with myself, the relative merits of pianists Gould, Brendel and Pollini (as I had once weighed the merits of Clapton, Hendrix and Harrison)? What was I doing standing outside Carnegie Hall on a bitterly cold afternoon scalping tickets for the hottest classical concert of the season, starring a diminutive visitor from another planet named Dudamel, when I had refused to do that for rock 'n roll shows, even for a Dylan? Or attending a recital on a steamy August afternoon on a barge under the Brooklyn Bridge? When Alex Ross of *The New Yorker*, author of a surprise bestseller on classical music, appeared on TV with Stephen Colbert, one blogger declared, "Classical music nerds around the world are now officially 8.4% cooler." Had I become one of those nerds? And was I now cooler or much less cool than when I was hanging out with Springsteen in New Jersey?

To be sure, I had listened to Beethoven, to a limited extent, before that. One could hardly grow up in the 1950s and early 1960s without some exposure to Leonard Bernstein and his Young People's Concerts, Van Cliburn on Ed Sullivan or Glenn Gould on *Omnibus*. Nearly anyone could identify the author of the first eight notes of the Fifth Symphony, but I never knew the source of the almost equally familiar opening to NBC's *Huntley-Brinkley* report (from the Ninth Symphony) or the most fanciful segment of Disney's *Fantasia* (from the Sixth Symphony). As a child, I did not play a musical instrument, and my awareness of classical music in general did not go much beyond *Peter and the Wolf* in the classroom and the *Nutcracker* on television, with the "William Tell" overture in the opening of *The Lone Ranger* a highlight.

Yet, from the age of four, music was my greatest love, even beyond baseball. I asked my parents to buy for me new singles by Tony Bennett and Eddie Fisher, and I entertained visitors by taking requests and spinning the 78s on my record player. Then rock 'n roll arrived, and like millions of other kids I became devoted to *American Bandstand* and Ricky Nelson playing his hits at the end of *Ozzie & Harriet*.

When Roy Orbison and then the Beatles and Bob Dylan emerged, followed by all the other great, late-'60s music, it ruled out any serious probing of that other "longhair" music. In his very electric "Tombstone Blues," Dylan claimed that "Ma Rainey and Beethoven once unwrapped their bed roll," but even this sexual imagery did not turn me on to Ludwig. Few of my peers showed any interest in classical music, beyond (for some) the Moody Blues' *Days of Future Past* recorded with the Royal Philharmonic or the hit single "Classical Gas." The Beatles were hailed by some classical composers for their use of strings on "Eleanor Rigby" but that sweetening left me cold. So did much of the first "rock opera," *Tommy* – it was overblown, like real opera. In my first review for *Rolling Stone* in 1970, I complained about the orchestration on Simon & Garfunkel's *Bridge Over Troubled Water*, and received a lot of hate mail for my troubles. The Strauss waltzes featured in *2001: A Space Odyssey* just bored me. So did the "Switched-On Bach" craze, led by Walter — before he became Wendy — Carlos, and I doubt it would have made any difference if it had been "Switched-on Beethoven."

Music was obviously still in my blood, however, and I threw away a promising career in mainstream journalism to serve as senior editor at the legendary rock magazine, *Crawdaddy* for nearly all of the 1970s. In those years, I had so much rock 'n roll to absorb (largely for free) there was no time for, or any interest in, pursuing other forms. Reggae was exotic enough, thank you, and I was too busy interviewing Ray Davies, Patti Smith and Frank Zappa and writing articles and reviews that would help make my new pal Bruce Springsteen a star — receiving a gold record from The Boss for *Born to Run* in appreciation.

Walter Carlos had returned to provide much of the soundtrack (including Beethoven snippets) for *A Clockwork Orange*, not my favorite Kubrick film but certainly popular among the *Crawdaddy* audience. You'll remember that the anti-hero of the film, Alex, liked to listen to a little "Ludwig van" before going out for some "ultra-violence" with his "droogies." A classical mini-boom followed, as record companies attempted to cash in on Kubrick by issuing samplers of great composers' work, with a nod to the drug culture: One series carried the titles *Mozart's Head, Prokofiev's Head,* and so forth, with trippy images on the album covers. *Crawdaddy* even unveiled a regular column "Going for Baroque," but it lasted only a year.   "Symphonic rock" had gone spandex, but I despised groups like Yes and Emerson, Lake and Palmer — even the more rocking Electric Light Orchestra, who had a hit with Chuck Berry's "Roll Over Beethoven." Walter Murphy's disco hit "A Fifth of Beethoven" might have turned me off to Ludwig forever.

In any event, that was about it, for me and classical music, until the mid-1980s. In general, I hoped I died before I got that old. Perhaps I had been exposed to Queen's "Bohemian Rhapsody" too many times. Out of *Crawdaddy* for a few years – and with no more free records or concert tickets coming my way — I was more open to classical music, and started purchasing the very occasional Mozart, Vivaldi or Bach recording. (Still, I remained oddly distant from the more scary Beethoven.) This dabbling, and no more, continued for two decades. Vivaldi in a church in Venice or Mozart in Paris were swell, but they didn't follow me home for long.

So, as the summer of my 60th birthday neared, I had never attended a classical performance in a large concert hall, still loathed opera (while remaining truly ignorant of it) and could not identify or even imagine the dozens of Beethoven masterpieces beyond the Fifth and Ninth symphonies, although surely I was exposed to the *Moonlight* sonata and snatches of other pieces in movie soundtracks and as Muzak at the supermarket. I had missed Gary Oldman's star turn as Beethoven in *Immortal Beloved*, not to mention the five Beethoven (the dog) movies. As editor of *Editor & Publisher*, a magazine known as the "bible of the newspaper industry," I had no professional contact with classical music, although we occasionally did raise the question, "How old is too old when it comes to rock critics?" At least I had escaped the rock 'n roll racket when I was still young.

Then one day I noticed the DVD for the film *Copying Beethoven*, starring Ed Harris, at the local video store.   My wife, equally in the dark on all things Beethoven, and I had considered catching the film when it hit the theaters, despite mixed reviews. We have a soft spot for historical and biographical dramas, but the movie soon disappeared.   Now we had a second chance.

We screen a lot of DVDs at home, but why this inauspicious one?   In retrospect, I believe the spark was set by a brief scene in my favorite movie of recent years, the Oscar-winning German drama, *The Lives of Others*.

The film depicts the East German secret police hounding a group of writers and actors just before the fall of the Berlin Wall. A playwright, who rightly suspects that intelligence agents have bugged his apartment, sits at the piano in his apartment and plays a very moving piece (written for the film) that brings tears to the eyes of a *Stasi* spy, upstairs in the same building, who is listening to it all on headphones.   The playwright explains to a friend that Lenin, the   Soviet leader, once said that he greatly admired Beethoven's piano sonata known as the *Appassionata*, but he had to stop listening to it because it was so profound it might prevent him from ordering the brutal steps he felt were needed to save his regime.

I'd never heard of the *Appassionata*, but the anecdote was so intriguing I vowed to investigate Beethoven, or perhaps even take the bold step (for me) of finding the sonata online. That determination faded, but the *Copying Beethoven* DVD brought it to mind again. There was another coincidental factor. My wife and I had just attended a Tanglewood concert in Lenox, Massachusetts, for the first time, at the invitation of my sister, for an all-Mozart program, and enjoyed the experience, even if "classical culture" seemed a little genteel. So many in the audience were older than we were, even used canes, walkers or wheelchairs. I couldn't decide if that was depressing or invigorating: to be out-geezered at a major musical event, for a change.

The truth was, I was bored with good old rock 'n roll. For months, I'd been listening to nothing but old favorites like Leonard Cohen, Professor Longhair, Townes Van Zandt and Richard Thompson. Nothing in recent literature particularly moved me; I had finished reading nearly all of Graham Greene, *Bleak House* and the entire *Don Quixote*. My son had gone off to college. After seven years in my current job, it was becoming routine, and the commute was starting to weigh on me. Probably I felt that Beethoven might represent fertile new ground, for I knew almost nothing about him beyond the deafness, and didn't even know when that set in or, for that matter, exactly when or where the great man lived. He might be a colossus, but one that had been hidden behind a mountain of other musical joys, and junk, my entire life.

That would change once I started watching *Copying Beethoven*. As critics had warned, the movie, directed by Agnieszka Holland, was a mixed blessing. Richard Roeper in his pan revealed that "the best movie about any Beethoven I've ever seen stars a Saint Bernard." Even those critical of the movie, however, had hailed an amazing ten-minute climax re-enacting the public debut of the Ninth Symphony in Vienna in April, 1824 – with Beethoven attempting to conduct while deaf.

The film portrayed a lovely young woman named Anna Holtz (Diane Kruger) hired out of the Vienna Conservatory to copy Beethoven's scores for the musicians. She overcomes his suspicions and hostility to help him "conduct" at the Ninth's debut, sitting in the orchestra pit and directing his motions. Ed Harris, with a wild head of hair – John Glenn in a fright wig – seemed far too American in the role; indeed, the role was intended for Anthony Hopkins. In the film, Beethoven's deafness (which in real-life was near-total in the time frame of the movie) seemed to come and go, like Mozart's giddy laugh in *Amadeus*. For some reason, Ludwig in his ramshackle apartment kept throwing buckets of water over himself. Was he crazy or did he have a dirt fetish (cleanliness next to his own godliness)? Harris performed Beethoven as bossy, self-indulgent, manipulative. It sounded right, for such an artist, but what did I know?

At least Anna Holtz didn't sleep with Ludwig or even try to, and in the end Beethoven inspires her to continue her own writing. There were striking scenes, such as Beethoven playing piano with an overhead rig that enabled him to at least hear the notes vibrating, and a deathbed scene accompanied by a truly haunting string quartet completely new to me. As promised, the Ninth Symphony premiere, though truncated, was spectacular. Despite the brutal edits, the music was considerably more exciting and moving than anything I'd heard by Mozart, Bach or Vivialdi, and then a few dozen voices lifted it to heaven. I realized I had not heard the entire choral finale for decades, beyond the "Ode to Joy," if ever.

That night, I marched down to my computer to search for some background on the Ninth. It turned out that Beethoven indeed had been allowed to "conduct" at the 1824 premiere, but from the side of the stage — and the orchestra had been advised to ignore him and only watch the real conductor. Beethoven stood there with a baton and marked the tempo for music he could not even hear. This much was true in the movie: Beethoven could not fathom the cascades of cheers at the close of the Ninth and a woman had turned him around so at least he could view the spectacle. Police had to be called to keep order. Then the composer was carried off on the shoulders of the crowd.

Yet reviews in the press back in 1824 were mixed: The damn thing was too long, the critics sniped, and why couldn't he just drop that interminable and misguided choral finale?

Beethoven, I learned from the web, had died in 1827, after years of great physical and emotional suffering, just three years after completing the Ninth. The legends about his passing were legion. In one his final words were, "Now the comedy ends"; in another he uttered, "I shall hear in heaven."   In a third version, a vast snow storm hit Vienna just as he was expiring and thunder cracked at his moment of death.   A fourth had him shaking a fist at the sky as lightning flashed, and when it fell back to the bed, he was dead. This much was not in dispute: More than 20,000 attended his funeral, an Elvis-sized tribute, considering the size of Vienna at the time.   Franz Schubert, who may or may not have met Beethoven, carried a torch in the parade (they are now buried nearly side-by-side).

I was surprised to learn that the Ninth had become so world famous so quickly. When Lincoln was assassinated in 1865, the New York Philharmonic suspended all concerts for a spell; returning, they chose the Ninth to mark the occasion, though they skipped the choral finale, claiming it was not appropriate (too much "joy" perhaps). After wide protests, the Philharmonic spokesman admitted the real reason for omitting the fourth movement was because it could not round up enough members for a large choir. Nearly a century later the funeral march from Beethoven's *Eroica* symphony was played for John F. Kennedy's funeral procession, and then as the key piece when the New York Philharmonic resumed performances after the assassination.

As for the Ninth today, I realized with some embarrassment that I did not know that the "Ode to Joy" now served as the official anthem of the European Union. Also, an original manuscript of this work had sold in 2003 for $3.3 million at Sotheby's. The head of Sotheby's manuscripts department, Dr. Stephen Roe, observed that the Ninth was "one of the highest achievements of man, ranking alongside *Hamlet* and *King Lear.*" Now a Norwegian sound artist had created an ultra-slow digital recording of the Ninth that lasts 24 hours, with pitch and timbre not affected.

The Ninth had almost a mystical impact. According to a Wikipedia entry, "Using modern numbering, several composers beside Beethoven have completed no more than nine symphonies. This has led certain subsequent composers, particularly

Gustav Mahler, to be superstitious about composing their own ninth or tenth symphonies, or to try to avoid writing them at all. This phenomenon has become known as the Curse of the Ninth."

But my favorite online discovery was this claim (disputed by many): The Ninth influenced the development of the compact disc. Sony devised a 10-cm diameter disc to hold one hour of music. Later, in 1979, a Sony executive (legend has it) insisted that a disc had to be large enough to contain the entire Ninth as conducted by Wilhelm Furtwangler in his famous 74-minute live 1951 recording. And so the width was increased to 12 cm, accommodating 80 minutes.

While absorbing all of this, I also searched for a strong version of the Ninth to download. I had no compass at all, virtually no knowledge of which orchestra or conductor was really "hot" right now. (I knew Bernstein had died and that was about it.) There were, of course, dozens of offerings for the Ninth at Amazon but I had no idea, for example, if the Philadelphia Orchestra (of Eugene Ormandy fame) was still any good. A recent release by the London Symphony Orchestra conducted by Bernard Haitink, whoever he was, was part of a Grammy-winning cycle, so that seemed like a safe bet. Five minutes later it was mine. No need to run out to Tower Records or the mall and maybe lose heart en route.

Soon, I was listening to it on my iPod on the commute to New York, every day. Even the first two movements, which could have sounded stale from overexposure (such as in the opening to Keith Olbermann's *Countdown* on MSNBC, where I was a frequent guest) leaped into my ears with fresh power. Then there was the choral finale, astonishing even in its operatic interludes.

To me, it was just as astonishing that I was astonished. I couldn't appreciate the music in technical terms – what was a *scherzo* or adagio? how did an oboe and bassoon differ? — but the emotional impact was profound, if mysterious. It struck a chord, but I didn't know yet what the chord was or where it was located, so I sought the observations of others. Furtwangler had offered a clue when he hailed Beethoven as "a whole musician, and beyond that, a saint and a visionary....It is this 'nostalgia of liberty' he feels, or better, makes us feel; this is what moves us to tears." Something was starting to do that for me, in any case.

Now it was full speed ahead, but to where? I had no idea what other Beethoven music to download. I ordered a pair of books about the Ninth via Amazon, one of them about its sometimes troubling political uses, especially by the Nazis (Furtwangler, perhaps unfairly, was labeled a Hitler sympathizer). Awaiting these books, I started combing the Web and standing in the stacks at Barnes and Noble at my lunch hour leafing through various bios and classical music guides.

There was, thankfully, general agreement on which dozen piano sonatas and which three piano concertos were the best, or at least most popular. At home I learned via Amazon which versions got the highest grades. Then I started searching for them on YouTube for a free listen, and after that downloading off iTunes and crossed my fingers. No need to worry. Glenn Gould's *Pastoral* piano sonata (shockingly jazzy in spots, as played by him), cello sonata #3 courtesy of YoYo Ma and Emanuel Ax, and Murray Perahia's *Emperor* piano concerto — they were all great. I'd keep going until a clunker gave me pause.

Now, what about experiencing the Ninth live for the first time? It would not be performed in New York City any time soon, but lo and behold in a few days it would close the Tanglewood season on a Sunday near the end of August, apparently a tradition.

Since the Mozart afternoon with my sister, I was no longer a Tanglewood virgin, but one problem remained. This concert would be presented not by the Boston Symphony (who were prepping for a European tour) but the Tanglewood Music Center Orchestra — young people studying there during the summer. This was apparently the first time they would be entrusted with this choice assignment. They would be under the direction of a world-class conductor, Rafael Fruhbeck de Burgos, but was this really the best way to start my Revolution No. 9? Only seats far on the side remained, but I was desperate, so we were soon set for my first Ninth.

While exploring the new electronic Beethoven delivery systems, I wondered: Can classical music from centuries ago offer a relief, an antidote, via the overwhelming be-here-now world of Blackberries, iTunes and the web? Alex Ross wrote in *The New Yorker* that classical music was "thriving on the Internet in unexpected ways," even beyond an explosion in the number of popular blogs following this subject. "News bulletins were declaring the classical-record business dead," Ross observed, "but I noticed strange spasms of life in the online CD and MP3 emporiums....

"The anonymity of Internet browsing has made classical music more accessible to non-fanatics; first-time listeners can read reviews, compare audio samples, and decide on, for example, a Beethoven recording by Wilhelm Furtwängler, all without risking the humiliation of mispronouncing the conductor's name under the sour gaze of a record clerk," Ross noted. "Likewise, first-time concertgoers and opera-goers can shop for tickets, study synopses of unfamiliar plots, listen to snippets of unfamiliar music, follow performers' blogs, and otherwise get their bearings on the lunar tundra of the classical experience..... For a little while the other day, a surprising name appeared at the top of Amazon.com's Top MP3 Artists, outperforming even Kanye West: Richard Wagner."

Ross concluded. "The classical business is not doing badly at present—and the unregulated openness of the Internet seems to have done it many favors. Perhaps no one should be surprised at this turn of events. If, as people say, the Internet is a paradise for geeks, it would logically work to the benefit of one of the most opulently geeky art forms in history."

In any case, for me, it was goodbye Crosby, Stills and Nash — hello Beaux Arts Trio!

Arriving at Tanglewood for the Ninth (after a three-hour drive), we were struck again by the massive crowd flush with oldsters. But on a bright Sunday summer afternoon, we also mingled with a large number of young couples, teens and kids out on the lawn in the $5 section. One hundred and eighty years after his death, Beethoven could still pack them in.

Our seats inside the "Shed" were close to the stage but far-left, giving us an odd, sideways look at the four primary singers and the conductor (meaning we could see his facial expressions), with two college-age timpanists directly above us threatening to explode the subtlety. When the choir filed in – the regulars in the Tanglewood Festival Chorus plus a couple of dozen students — and took their places on the bleachers, I could hardly wait for them to sing (knowing it wouldn't happen for almost an hour into the Ninth).

Having never heard the Ninth, or nearly any other symphony, performed live, it was hard to judge the youthful playing. It seemed fine to me and conductor de Burgos did not grimace often. The opening, tentative notes of the first movement (almost like the orchestra merely warming up) provoked an emotional rush, and my skin tingled off and on throughout the first movement. The second movement *scherzo* galloped along enjoyably, but the *adagio* dragged, as I had not yet unlocked its secrets. Then the final movement arrived with all of its stupendous power, and finally the singers rose as one for the "Ode to Joy" and so much more. This portion of the titanic Ninth Symphony might be considered the anthem of the planet Earth, I decided. And I had missed most of it for my entire life.

As the assembled voices peaked, and then peaked impossibly again, I sensed this would be one of the most fateful musical afternoons of my life. And all this with a junior varsity orchestra. The crowd went wild. I could imagine many a tear flowing from many a proud parent—and player. I could barely contain my own. After just a few weeks in these new waters, I had come to agree with the pianist Louis Kentner, when he declared that Beethoven's creations should be presented to the first Martian visitor to our planet as proof of what our civilization is capable of. Here, friend, we would say to the little green men: This is the best of us.

Leon Botstein, the president of Bard College and well-known conductor, had written in the *Wall Street Journal*: "Classical music has always appealed to older adults who, with the passing of years, tend to contemplate the life conundrums that are freighted with ambiguity and complexity....The challenge facing classical musicians is to persuade adults to listen, even those who have no experience with classical music." Well, I seemed to be meeting this challenge at last, but for how long?

CHAPTER SEVEN

A Life of "Sufferings and Joys"

The wide-ranging facts and trivia surrounding Beethoven's legacy and cultural impact that I gleaned from surfing the Web after returning from Tanglewood often proved overwhelming, coming at me in a haphazard, non-chronological fashion. The Beatles' song "Because" was based on the chord pattern of the *Moonlight* sonata played backwards, and "Ode to Joy" turns up at several points in their movie *Help*. Scientists in South Korea claimed that playing the *Moonlight* inspired rice crops to grow faster. A lock of Beethoven's hair had been auctioned not long ago and the winning bidders then ordered a DNA test to try to prove why he died (it suggested lead poisoning as the culprit).

The famous opening notes of the Fifth Symphony, *dum-dum-dum-DUM,* were used as a signature piece for the Allies on radio during World War II, since the notes were Morse Code for the letter "V" (for "Victory"). Michael Jackson had to pay royalties to the Cleveland Symphony after "sampling" the Ninth on a hit album. And so on. My wife shared much of my enthusiasm, and often forwarded esoterica I had missed.

From the Beethoven biographies I had torn through, I finally gained a fuller sense of his life.

Born in Bonn in 1770, he studied first with his abusive and alcoholic father, Johann, a singer and instrumentalist who pushed for him to be recognized as a child prodigy, like Mozart. While not quite at that level, he did survive a troubled and modest upbringing to become the greatest pianist in Bonn as a teen. In a visit to Vienna, the biographers suggested, he either did (or did not) have a brief meeting with Mozart, who either was (or was not) impressed. The most favorable view has Mozart, who would soon pass away, commenting, "Keep your eye on this lad. Some day he will give the world something to talk about." In any case, Beethoven likely would have become a student of Mozart's if he hadn't been called back to Bonn because of his beloved mother's illness; she would die when he was sixteen.

In 1792, Beethoven settled in Vienna, and pursued his studies, mainly with an aging Haydn, then considered the greatest composer in Europe but often mocked by the ambitious pupil for being stuck in time. Beethoven soon found patrons among the music-mad Viennese aristocracy. At nineteen, he wrote his first masterpiece, a cantata for the funeral of Emperor Joseph. In a sign of things to come, the cantata was never performed, deemed too difficult for the singers and musicians. The composer, however, would make use of its stunning aria much later in his sole opera, *Fidelio*.

Beethoven was not an imposing or attractive figure, no matter what some of the artists who drew or painted him suggested in their flattery: fairly short, a little stocky, with a dark complexion that produced rumors that he was part black, with Spanish Moor bloodlines. This was a claim embraced by some black leaders (such as Malcolm X) and academics during the 1960s, recently updated in a short story by Nadine Gordimer, "Beethoven Was One-Sixteenth Black." Ludwig had a lot to overcome, not the least the fact that high-level composers were expected to emerge from the aristocracy or at least have some noble blood, which he resented and battled (often in embarrassing scenes) all of his life. Beethoven added the "van" to his name and claimed that he hailed from a privileged background, and even planted rumors that he was the illegitimate son of a prince, all false.

From his mid-twenties, Beethoven began turning out startling works in several forms, including piano sonatas (including the *Moonlight* and *Pathetique*), piano concertos, and his first two symphonies. Unlike most composers, he earned a steady income outside the palaces. The sheet music of his piano sonatas sold widely, the equivalent of "hit singles" in popular music today; a handful he churned out to produce what we now call "product." Few might have attended his live performances but he became known, and his music played, from England to Italy.

His personal life remained stormy, with ill-fated

love affairs (he never came close to marrying) and various physical ailments the norm. Soon he noticed that he was starting to lose his hearing, though he kept this a secret from nearly everyone. "Imagine this happening to me – of all people," he muttered to one associate, who could only nod at what must be one of the great understatements in all of recorded history. According to several accounts, he first noticed the hearing loss on a walk in the countryside (one of his favorite pastimes) when a friend remarked on the beauty of a song a shepherd was singing in the field. Beethoven could not hear it at all. In one of the many supremely haunting aspects of Beethoven's life, he would, just a little later, write for his *Pastoral* symphony a sublime movement titled "Shepherd's Song."

Actually, his hearing crisis was even worse than this suggests. He wrote to one friend that his ears were filled with "buzzing" or ringing even while he tried to compose or sleep – what we would identify now as the coming of "tinnitus." So any image of Beethoven composing in silence (hard enough) needs to be set aside and replaced with the true horror.

In 1802, even as he reached the first peak of his writing prowess, he pondered suicide when he recognized that his growing deafness was likely incurable. That autumn, at a village outside Vienna, he wrote the *Heiligenstadt Testament*, addressed to his two brothers, describing his bitter unhappiness over his affliction — "You do not know the secret cause" and now he was "compelled to face the prospect of a lasting malady" — and hinting he would soon take his life. "Ah," he wrote, "how could I possibly admit an infirmity in the one sense which ought to be more perfect in me than in others?" and adding, "I must live almost alone, like one who has been banished." One of the most moving documents ever written by a famous artist, it was discovered only after his death a quarter century later.

But he came through this period with his determination intact and entered a new creative phase, generally called his "middle period." It was characterized by a heroic tone, especially evident in the revolutionary Third (*Eroica*) Symphony — after attending its premiere, Haydn, his former teacher, said, "After this, nothing is the same" — and Fifth Symphony. It also dominated his other work, such as his *Appasionata* piano sonata, *Emperor* piano concerto, *Archduke* trio and *Kreutzer* violin sonata, and his opera *Fidelio*. The famous opening notes of the Fifth Symphony were said to be inspired by a knock on his door — "fate knocking." That fit the heroic image, but others swear that he once testified he was merely copying the chirping of a bird.

Beethoven became the most famous composer in the world, but lived fitfully, frequently moving from one apartment to another, suffering from personal tragedies and debts as his hearing worsened. He signed "exclusive" publishing deals for his works — with multiple companies. Often irascible, but at other times warm and entertaining, he might have been what we now call "bipolar," or perhaps it was more a sign of failing hearing. After several public humiliations, when he banged away in an ugly fashion, he could no longer play the piano for others. Beethoven started using a special rod attached to the soundboard on a piano that he could bite — the vibrations would then transfer from the piano to his jaw to increase his perception of the sound. He also collected ear "horns" for conversing in public, but he began shunning most social engagements due to his handicap.

Politically, he was an idealist and democrat who favored personal freedoms and policies that favored the average folk. Even when he took commissions and favors from princes and aristocrats, he had trouble interacting with them. He generally refused to sit down at the piano and play, like a trained seal, at parties for the well-connected. Yet he had a weakness for rulers who wielded power on behalf of the poor, and originally dedicated the *Eroica* to Napoleon. Then, when he learned that Bonaparte had made himself emperor, he removed the dedication — the manuscript for the symphony that survives today carries deep angry scratches where he removed the emperor's name.

The unhappy attempts at romance continued, usually with women high above his station or married — or a young pupil — and in 1812 he wrote a now-famous letter addressed only to his "immortal beloved" that has inspired nearly two centuries of detective work, not to mention countless books, poems, academic treatises and movies. The woman, whoever she was, had drawn Beethoven's ardor and obviously had returned it, but there was something illicit about it, most likely, she was married. At least half a dozen semi-plausible suspects have surfaced. Beethoven's note revealed deep passion, but also ambivalence. It may not have even been delivered, or perhaps he was thoroughly thwarted, nothing new for him.

In any case, his attempts at romance pretty much

ended with this rejection or failure to act. It remains one of the great romantic mysteries in history.

Starting in 1815 he became embroiled in a rather sordid attempt to win custody of his beloved nephew Karl, after Ludwig's brother died suddenly, and this apparently helped cause the first creative dry spell of his career. With no child of his own, and dwindling hope for one, Beethoven considered Karl his own son and tried to take him away (through legal and other means) from his widowed mother. For months at a time the boy lived with Beethoven but court rulings often went against the composer—and in the process it became public knowledge that he had cooked up the "van" in his name, another humiliation. Finally sent off to boarding school, Karl tried to take his own life but a pistol shot barely missed his brain. He survived and reconciled with Beethoven at the end.

Coming out of that crisis, and now completely deaf—he communicated with others mainly via a sketchbook—Beethoven would write his most profound and innovative music in his final years, one of the few composers to accomplish a late-life renewal on this scale. Indeed, it was music never heard before, both supremely lyrical and, at times, almost atonal. Decades later, Stravinsky would suggest that Beethoven invented 20th century music, in the 1820s. The output included his greatest piano sonatas (numbers 30 to 32) and his five late violin quartets, which included some of the most magisterial pieces of art ever created. Then there was his supreme religious offering, the *Missa Solemnis* (he was no churchgoer but did believe in God and heaven), and, of course, his Ninth Symphony.

"We mortals with immortal minds are only born

for sufferings and joys," Beethoven wrote in a sketchbook at this time, "and one could almost say that the most excellent receive joy through sufferings." And: "Music is the one incorporeal entrance into the higher world of knowledge which comprehends mankind but which mankind cannot comprehend."

Maynard Solomon, in his book on Beethoven's later years, described "a sweeping realignment of his understanding of nature, divinity, and human purpose, constituting a sea change in Beethoven's system of beliefs."

For Beethoven, the act of composition had always been a struggle, as the scrawls on his composition papers and sketchbooks show. But in these late works, as Edward Said has noted, the sense of "isolation" is complete — though Said's friend, the pianist Daniel Barenboim, disagreed with him on that word, saying "desolation" fit better. In any case, the sense of agonizing effort is a part of the music, and the legend. Yet, as in Van Gogh's case, the legend proves justified and holds up to deep reflection today.

Beethoven's final months were even more horrid than much of what preceded them. Three times a doctor punctured his abdomen to release gallons of liquid. A steady line of friends and fellow musicians came to pay their last respects. When one brought an expensive bottle of wine, he said only, "Too late, alas, too late."

Beethoven died in 1827 at the age of fifty-six. An unprecedented crowd attended the funeral in Vienna. The orator at his grave declared: "He withdrew from his fellow men after he had given them everything and had received nothing in return. He remained alone because he found no second self. But until his death he preserved a human heart for all men, a father's heart for his own people, the whole world." He added, with words that I could suddenly, and surprisingly, now comprehend: "Whenever, during your lives, the power of his works overwhelms you like a coming storm; when your rapture pours out in the midst of a generation yet unborn; then remember this hour and think: we were there when they buried him, and when he died we wept!"

After his death, several friends or family members snipped locks of his hair. An autopsy was inconclusive as to cause of death, giving rise to more mysteries and theories, with the culprits ranging from alcoholism to syphilis (they are generally disregarded today). In one view, doctors essentially killed him through mistreatment or poor hygiene in the draining of his abdomen. And the lead poisoning claim? Explanations for this have ranged from the lead pipes used for Vienna's water supply to the treatment of his stomach punctures with poultices that included lead. But one finding has endured: His ear canals were found to be so withered that the diagnosis of tinnitus appears to be tragically accurate. Thankfully, it is likely that the buzzing stopped in his final years when stone deafness arrived.

In a disturbing twist that followed his death, his longtime assistant Anton Schindler spirited away many of Beethoven's personal belongings and sold them. Schindler did retain hundreds of his conversation books, but forged writings on some of them to make himself and/or the great man look better. Then he wrote a biography based on some of this fiction—which unfortunately stood as a respected source for decades.

In America, Beethoven had slowly found renown, but this grew greatly after his death. Transcendentalist and early feminist Margaret Fuller considered him her "hero," wrote letters to him (even after his passing), and declared, "Beethoven seems to have chronicled all the sobs, the heart-heavings, and godlike Promethean thefts of the Earth-Spirit."

And there was this amazing thing: A little more than a decade after his death there was already talk of his Ninth Symphony as the European anthem. A July 1837 article in *Musical World* cited "the universal Hallelujah" of the "Ode to Joy." The writer questioned why a proposed monument to Beethoven—a rarity for any musician or composer at the time — should be erected in Bonn and not in, say, London at St. Paul's or Westminster Abbey. "After all," he pointed out, "the greatest monument Beethoven can have is the proper performance of his works: the annual repetition of the choral symphony by 1000 or 1500 persons—the grand masonic hymn of Europe borne up by 1000 voices, and supported by an orchestra of 500 instrumentalists, would be the apotheosis which even the composer would have desired for an extension of his thread of life to have witnessed."

CHAPTER EIGHT

The Obsession

Those early iTunes downloads left me hungry for more, but I was also intimidated by so much more to explore. Thank god Beethoven wasn't as prolific as Mozart or Bach. In the days ahead, I started sampling musical configurations I hardly knew existed before: "trios" (add the violin to a cello and piano), a triple concerto (those three instruments plus orchestra), a "septet" and so forth. At the same time, I noticed that I was starting to lose my own hearing. No doubt my early years of attending dozens of rock 'n roll shows every year, with seats close to the stage (thanks to my magazine credentials), had come back to haunt me. Now, ironically, listening to Beethoven on my iPod at high volume was adding to the damage. So that is what I had to cope with during this intense exposure to the most famous hearing-impaired artist ever.

One night that autumn I was leafing through that week's *New Yorker* and spotted a stunning black and white photograph of two young, attractive, musicians set to appear at the Metropolitan Museum's concert stage in about a week, playing all five of Beethoven's cello sonatas. The pianist, Simone Dinnerstein, currently had a bestselling CD of Bach's *Goldberg Variations*. The cellist was Zuill Bailey. Miraculously, the Met still had a few seats left in the balcony. Was I retreating to, or hurtling toward, a completely different country: the nation of Beethoven? And this, I knew, was barely the beginning of the journey.

My new obsession surged in the weeks ahead, as I downloaded a dozen CDs, purchased several books, viewed countless videos on YouTube, and rented the DVD for *Immortal Beloved*, with its screwball theory on the ID of the mystery lover: Ludwig's hated sister-in-law, with nephew Karl actually his love child! Yet I was, in some ways, saving the best for last, holding back on the difficult late piano sonatas and late quartets, and the *Missa Solemnis*. Early favorites continued to hold sway, especially the slow movements, as in the *Archduke* and *Ghost* trios, the violin concerto, the *Emperor* piano concerto, *Spring* violin sonata, Seventh Symphony, and so on.

What Beethoven shared with the greatest rock stars, I had learned, was his constant drive to top himself, to keep pushing the envelope, to finish epic pieces with a universe-cracking chord or sustained single note. And to think I once thought that was reserved for "We Won't Get Fooled Again." What also made Beethoven so appealing for me was that, politically, he was an idealist and democrat, and it went beyond the message of the Ninth ("all men become brothers"), as explored in Part I of this book. Even when he took commissions and favors from princes and aristocrats, he blasted the autocracy.

My new self did something unthinkable just a few weeks earlier: I attended a weekday afternoon lecture at the Met, on Beethoven's middle period. It was pretty much me and several dozen elderly ladies-who-lunch.

Then there were the live performances. I returned to the Met for the Dinnerstein-Bailey cello sonata marathon, my first Beethoven concert ever in an auditorium setting. Then I made it to Avery Fisher for the first time since the 1974 Springsteen concert, when it was still called Philharmonic Hall. Part of the stage extension collapsed that night under the weight of the foot-stomping Boss. (It was also my only night backstage in that venue.) Even that didn't top the night in 1971 when, at the same site, I watched an inebriated Ray Davies of the Kinks fall backward — and his feuding brother, guitarist Dave Davies, let an amp topple over, nearly bonking Ray on the head.

Now, on this night, Paul Lewis and the London Symphony with Sir Colin Davis at the helm offered a stunning Piano Concerto No.4, especially the haunting middle movement, which some say portrays the Orpheus legend. When it was over, I turned to my wife and whispered, "Not bad for an opening act." We spent the intermission walking the corridors, generally enjoying the high-culture vibe and looking at historic photographs, even finding a picture of a guy we know in our hometown, Joseph Alessi, trombonist for the New York Philharmonic (I had coached his son in Little League). Then, after intermission: a towering *Eroica*.

So I'd made my triumphant return to Philharmonic Hall. A few days later, I paid another return visit – this time to Carnegie Hall. The last time it was for a rock concert with patrons smoking pot and putting out cigarettes on the carpeted floor. During the 1970s, I attended shows there by Neil Young, Van Morrison, Carole King, Bill Withers, Bonnie Raitt, Willie Nelson and others. Now it was for the renowned St. Petersburg Orchestra, with young Julia Fischer performing Beethoven's only violin concerto.

First thing we saw, entering this tidy cathedral, was a long line of elderly folks waiting for an elevator to carry them up to the dress circle. Boy, back in the day, they either didn't have that or no self-respecting young rock fan would ever climb aboard. Of course, I was impressed by the renovations, the lack of burn holes in the arm rests, the general air of class so missing in my many long ago visits. And the concert was thrilling, besides.

Carrying obsession to an extreme enabled by modern technology, I checked Google News several times a day for new Beethoven mentions from around the world. There I learned, for example, that the Baltimore Symphony had launched a fascinating series of concerts, promoted via NPR, called "Beethoven CSI," a musical and medical exploration of his hearing loss and cause of death.

Also this: Beethoven in a letter had responded to

a request from his friend and patron Archduke Rudolph: "I notice that your Imperial Highness wishes to make an experiment on horses by means of my music. It is to see, so I perceive, whether the riders thereby can make some clever somersaults. Ha ha, I must really laugh at your Imperial Highness thinking of me in this matter; for that I shall be to the end of my life. N.B. — The desired horse-music will reach your Imperial Highness at full gallop." Sure enough, he soon sent along a march.

Finally I learned the inspiration for "Roll Over Beethoven": Chuck Berry's sister hogging the piano to play classical music when he was a kid. That, he explained, "delayed rock 'n roll for twenty years." Charles Schulz, creator of *Peanuts*, frequently featured Beethoven — even notes from some of his pieces — in the comic strip, but he confessed he actually favored Brahms (the name Beethoven worked better visually). I did not know the intro to *Everybody Loves Raymond* carried a snippet of the "Ode to Joy," while *Judge Judy* used the opening of the Fifth Symphony to announce rulings from the bench. Somehow I had also missed an apparently famous TV commercial starring one of my faves, Elvis Costello, sitting in the back seat of a Lexus, listening to the *scherzo* of the Ninth while explaining that Beethoven did write "a few toe-tappers."

Frank Lloyd Wright, I learned, was a huge Beethoven fan, hailing the composer as a great motif architect and "builder." The Fifth Symphony, he said, was "a great symphonic poem that is probably the noblest thought-built edifice in the world."

Then there was this wonderful anecdote: When the Steinway Musical Instruments company went public in 1996, they discovered that SMI was already taken for use at the New York Stock Exchange. So what did they choose? LVB.

Meanwhile, I bought the CD for Furtwangler's epic 1951 performance of the Ninth. Finally I got hooked on the *adagio* (the least-famous of the four movements), which in Furtwangler's stately version went on and on. For good measure, I rented the DVD of the 2001 movie *Taking Sides*, directed by Istvan Szabo and starring Stellan Skarsgard as the conductor. Based on a play, it's a fascinating portrait of a postwar American military investigator (Harvey Keitel) probing Furtwangler's relationship with the Nazis, with the conductor claiming, half-convincingly, that he resisted as much as possible, and even helped some Jewish musicians to escape.

Of special interest in the film was the central role played by the infamous performance of the Ninth by the Berlin Philharmonic, conducted by Furtwangler, to mark Hitler's birthday. I'd already watched the short video on YouTube, which shows Nazi leaders such as Goebbels and Goering in the audience (Hitler was a no-show). Debate continues over what happened at the end. It appears that Furtwangler, after warily shaking the hand of Goebbels, transfers a handkerchief from his left hand to his right as if to remove the stain. Or maybe he just wanted to wipe away some sweat. The movie ended with a grainy clip of that moment, without clarifying it.

Further digging uncovered numerous other movies, often from abroad, that touched on Beethoven. One I'd have to track down was an early Ingmar Bergman film, *To Joy*, which profiles a conductor and violinist preparing to play the Ninth.

By now, I had discovered, via iTunes, Glenn Gould's version of Liszt's transcription of the *Pastoral* symphony — he took the trouble to transcribe all of the symphonies for piano — and listened to it on the train commuting to and from New York, almost every day, sometimes with tears in my eyes (on the subway, no less). Vladimir Horowitz, near the end of his life, professed to only two regrets: not becoming a composer, and never recording the Lizst/Beethoven transcriptions. 'These are the greatest works for the piano, tremendous works," he declared. "But they are 'sound' works. For me, the piano is the orchestra. I don't like the sound of piano as a piano. I like to imitate the orchestra — the oboe, the clarinet, the violin, and, of course, the singing voice. Every note of those symphonies is in these Liszt works."

I even bought my wife a Nano so she could enjoy some of my downloads. We both got hooked on podcasts of pianist Andras Schiff's recent lectures in London on all 32 sonatas, and for good measure purchased tickets for him playing four of them at Carnegie Hall the following April. And there were more books: from the legacy of Beethoven's hair to a Vikram Seth novel about a quarreling string quartet set in London.

Leonard Bernstein's *Art of Music* opened with his imagined dialogue with a friend, on a long car trip, citing Beethoven's shortcomings—with Lenny declaring that, no matter, he was still our greatest composer, no question. Bernstein wrote, "Many, many composers have been able to write heavenly tunes and respectable fugues. Some composers can orchestrate the C-major scale so that it sounds like a masterpiece, or fool with notes so that a harmonic novelty is achieved. But this is all mere dust—nothing compared to the magic ingredient sought by them all: the inexplicable ability to know what the next note has to be. Beethoven had this gift in a degree that leaves them all panting in the rear guard.

"Beethoven broke all the rules, and turned out pieces of breath-taking rightness. Rightness—that's the word! When you get the feeling that whatever note succeeds the last is the only possible note that can rightly happen at that instant, in that context, then chances are you're listening to Beethoven. Melodies, fugues, rhythms—leave them to the Tchaikovskys and Hindemiths and Ravels. Our boy has the real goods, the stuff from Heaven, the power to make you feel at the finish: Something is right in the world. There is something that checks throughout, that follows its own law consistently: something we can trust, that will never let us down."

When the friend points out that this is almost the "definition of God," Bernstein replies: "I meant it to be."

As time passed, my fascination with Beethoven spilled over more and more from the musical to the visual, and I don't mean merely to attractive performers like French pianist Helene Grimaud. Remember, my introduction to Beethoven that year had been sparked by two films, one great, one not so much: *The Lives of Others* and *Copying Beethoven*. After watching the often preposterous *Immortal Beloved*, I almost stopped right there, but instead plunged on.

And what a film festival. There was a silent short,

a 1930s Abel Gance feature starring an actor later tortured and killed by the Gestapo, and a Disney film. A classic children's story — and a ridiculous biopic by former Warhol director Paul Morrissey. Numerous documentaries and docudramas. And then there was the "Ludwig van" of *A Clockwork Orange*. (For a full round-up see the Appendix at the close of this book.)

Three months after the start of my journey with Beethoven, the Venezuelan wunderkind Gustavo Dudamel came to Carnegie Hall with his Simon Bolivar Youth Orchestra. He had just been picked to take over the Los Angeles Philharmonic, and *The New York Times* had declared that "Dudamelmania" was breaking out wherever he appeared. This was one of the toughest tickets in town, but I managed to score a single balcony ticket online and would try to scalp a second ticket outside. If unsuccessful, my wife and I would flip a coin to see who would attend.

Scalping outside Carnegie! This had a rich rock 'n roll tradition from back in the 1970s but I had no idea if this practice existed for classical concerts. Happily, around the corner from the front entrance, I found a well-dressed, middle-aged guy selling an "extra" ticket in the dress circle. He bore no resemblance to the scuzzy rock 'n roll scalpers I knew from my youth. Perhaps his wife simply got sick — but if so, why did he have several other tickets in his pocket?

In any case, the concert was a smash, my first live experience of Beethoven's Fifth, and Dudamel certainly nailed the resounding final movement. Then, as the audience went crazy - with some of them waving Venezuelan flags in the balcony - he brought his kids back, dressed in satin jackets, to perform, dancing around the stage while playing selections from *West Side Story*. But WWLT (what would Ludwig think)? Well, maybe he'd love it. "Music is a higher revelation than all wisdom and philosophy," Beethoven once boasted, "it is the wine of a new procreation, and I am Bacchus who presses out this glorious wine for men and makes them drunk with the spirit."

By then, I'd decide to spend part of my 60th birthday in the company of Beethoven — that is, with the great French pianist Pierre-Laurent Aimard performing the 3rd piano concerto with the New York Philharmonic, even though it started at 11 a.m. Linked to that, Aimard and fellow pianist Emanuel "Manny" Ax were to chat about Beethoven at the John Jay College auditorium in New York. Naturally, I was there.

The two men sat on chairs on stage, each dressed in casual black sport coats and open-necked shirts-- Aimard suave, Ax pudgy, a *mensch* — next to a host who tossed them softball questions, which they answered with great enthusiasm. Aimard called Beethoven an "architect...he had such a sense of what's right...He can be so adventurous because he can always find the right balance, always injecting something from another galaxy. He brings in the whole universe" and presents ideas in "completely strange ways," from "another dimension."

Ax: "He was a great dramatist, so theatrical." And: "What's so amazing about Beethoven is his ability to handle time. Everything seems to last exactly the right time and everything seems just right wherever you are in the piece, yet you are aware of the passage of time."

When talk turned to the 4th piano concerto, the men ambled to twin pianos nearby and played a thrilling call and response (with Ax taking the part of the orchestra) from the second movement. Then they played a bit from the 3rd concerto.

Someone from the audience asked if they thought Beethoven had any weaknesses. They both laughed, as if to say, are you nuts? Ax said that it reminded him of that George Bush press conference when he was asked if he had made any mistakes and Bush said he couldn't think of any. Aimard finally volunteered that some early works have a lot of "repeats," unlike LvB's final sonatas and string quartets, which are "wholly inventive, new forms of composition." Ax added, "Yes, some pieces are complete innovations, and others are just....fabulous pieces!"

Two days later my 60th birthday arrived, with Aimard navigating a dynamic Piano Concerto No.3. After lunch, my wife and I visited the Morgan Library for a display of Van Gogh's original letters. The artist as a young man had commented on Beethoven in a 1884 letter to brother Theo: "Dupré is perhaps even more of a colourist than Corot and Daubigny, although they both are too, and Daubigny really is very daring in colours. But with Dupré there's something of a magnificent symphony in the colour, carried through, intended, manly. I imagine Beethoven must be something like that. This symphony is surprisingly CALCULATED and yet simple and infinitely deep, like nature itself. That's what I think about it — about Dupré. "

And then, from the asylum at St. Remy not long

before his death, he commented in another letter to Theo, "We painters are always asked to compose ourselves and to be nothing but composers. Very well – but in music it isn't so – and if such a person plays some Beethoven he'll add his personal interpretation to it – in music, and then above all for singing – a composer's interpretation is something, and it isn't a hard and fast rule that only the composer plays his own compositions."

Closing out the day, we headed to Tarrytown, across the river from our home, for dinner. Walking to our car afterward on Main Street, we passed an ethnic food shop run by a man born in Morocco, which had just closed for the night. Blasting from inside as the staffers cleaned and carted: the Beethoven violin concerto. We could only stand outside and laugh.

That was it for concerts for awhile, owing to the usual holiday lull. I read Maynard Solomon's much-honored biography. New, if relatively obscure, Beethoven wonders continued to emerge for me: his surprising settings of Scottish folk songs; his "Choral Fantasy," with a melodic precursor of the "Ode to Joy"; and *An die ferne Geliebte*, the first true song-cycle anyone ever wrote.

Daniel Barenboim's traversal of the 32 piano sonatas, judging from the press coverage in London, represented the musical event of the century there. This sparked my own Barenboim frenzy, catching up on his writing about, and with, the noted intellectual Edward Said (another Beethoven champion and a pretty fair pianist himself) and their admirable work with the Israeli-Palestinian orchestra, the West-East

Divan. I found I could relate completely to Barenboim's explanation for his own Beethoven devotion: "I think that there is a very important personal message in each one of the Beethoven pieces...How free is the human being? How does the human being deal with himself? How does he deal with his problems of existence? How does he see himself? How does he cope with his anxieties, with anguish? How does he cope with joy? How does he cope with all those things? All that, and much more, is for me the substance of Beethoven."

This also led me to music, videos and writings related to his late wife, Jacqueline du Pre, who had recorded with Barenboim the Beethoven cello sonatas and piano trios. I even rented the so-so *Hillary and Jackie* movie drama starring Emily Watson and Rachel Griffiths.

While still biding my time before plunging into the string quartets, I was already overcome by the slow movement in the opus 132 quartet, which Beethoven had labeled the *Heiliger Dankgesang*. Its sixteen minutes of unearthly beauty can spark primal emotions especially if you know that it was written to celebrate surviving one of his near-fatal health crises. It is titled, in German, "Holy Song of Thanksgiving by a Convalescent to the Divinity," with its two sprightly passages marked on the manuscript, "Feeling New Strength." Now I recognized that this was what had so memorably closed *Copying Beethoven* in the death-bed scene. I'd found this quote from Basil Lam's 1975 book, *Beethoven String Quartets*: "[A]t the end the 6/3 chord of C major quietly dismisses modern tonality; what remains is either the most authentic spiritual illumination in music, or the incomprehensible abstract of a genius out of touch with reality. "

When the Edmund Morris lecture arrived, I sat in the front row, and heard him reveal, "Beethoven saved my life. Literally." It seems that as a boy, growing up in Kenya, his father put on a record of the *Appassionata* one day and his dad turned the lights out to listen to it. Morris, then 14, was so "pole-axed" by the music he could not move when asked to get up to turn the lights on. So his father did it — and saw a six-foot cobra at his son's feet. "If I had gotten up and stepped on it, I wouldn't be here today," he told us. "So thank you, Beethoven, for making this evening possible."

He also asserted, "Of all the great composers, Beethoven is the most enduring in his appeal to dilettantes and intellectuals alike. What draws them is Beethoven's universality, his ability to embrace the whole range of human emotion, from dread of death to love of life—and the metaphysics beyond— reconciling all doubts and conflicts in a catharsis of sound."

Unimaginable just a few months before: I had the courage to ask a question from the audience about the *Heiliger Dankgesang,* the first German I'd spoken since middle school.

More concerts followed, including the magical Helene Grimaud doing the 5th piano concerto at Carnegie (on Super Bowl Sunday, but who cares?) and the 4th at Avery Fisher. By now, I was taking new Beethoven pieces in stride. One thing I'd learned at the outset was: don't be intimidated. What makes Beethoven so "universal" (besides being

127

played and listened to in every corner of the globe) is that his music has something for everyone. It can almost convince an atheist that God exists, or even that Beethoven is God.

Illustrating this was an NPR interview in which Scott Simon asked Said and Barenboim about their shared passion for Beethoven.

SAID: "Beethoven in the first place really transcends the time and place of which he was a part. I mean, he's an Austro-Germanic composer who speaks to anyone who likes music, no matter whether that person is African or Middle Eastern or American or European. And that extraordinary accomplishment is entirely due to this music of striving and development and of somehow expressing the highest human ideals: ideals of brotherhood, of community, of yearning; perhaps in many instances, unfulfilled yearning. But these are universal experiences. And part of its great appeal is that it's wordless, you know, so you can in a sense formulate what you want to go into it."

BARENBOIM: "What Edward has said is that the most extraordinary element in Beethoven is that in so many of his works, he seems to be purposely creating a feeling of disorder or chaos or not really knowing exactly where you are harmonically, for instance, and in many other ways, too, in order to then, through a process of strife and musical development...to find order out of the chaos. And I think this is what gives the music such humanity."

When Said died in September 2003 (his final essay was on Beethoven and "late style"), Barenboim wrote for *Time* magazine, "He fought for Palestinian rights while understanding Jewish suffering, and did not see this posture as a paradox. We founded the West-East Divan as a forum where young Israeli and Arab musicians understood that before Beethoven we all stand as equals. "

Besides that, what I found vital was this: Thanks to his relative lack of production, it was surprisingly easy to identify and explore the Beethoven universe. It's quality, not quantity, and you rarely come upon a real stinker – in contrast to, say, the Dylan or Van Morrison *oeuvre* – that might discourage further exploration. If anything, the deeper I plunged, the more enthralled I became.

I also appreciated the arc to Beethoven's output. He never was "over the hill"; he stood right at the peak near the very end, with works that, as Schubert famously complained, "left us nothing left to write." His final symphony, mass, piano sonatas and quartets are considered by many the Himalayas of Western music. Edward Said put it this way: "It is as if the earlier extrovert has turned inward, and now produces gnarled and eccentric pieces of music that make unprecedented demands on performer and listener alike, and at the same time convey a sense not of resignation but of an unusual rebelliousness, breaking barriers, transgressively exploring the basic elements of the art as if anew."

In Thomas Mann's *Doctor Faustus*, Adrian Leverkühn's composition teacher, Wendell Kretschmar, gives a lecture in which he says, "Beethoven's art had overgrown itself, risen out of the habitable regions of tradition, even before the startled gaze of human eyes, into spheres of the entirely and utterly and nothing but personal – an ego painfully isolated in the absolute, isolated too from sense by the loss of his hearing..."

But all of this does not quite explain why I came so completely under the spell of Beethoven. One non-musical aspect surely was that, as with Van Gogh, the troubled life and heroic struggles of Beethoven shape appreciation of the art he produced while deepening the emotional attachment to it. Like Van Gogh's paintings, Beethoven's music could stand on its own, but understanding the effort and pain that went into it – knowing the chronology of his life and the specific inspiration for many pieces – makes it reach a far deeper place. It's one reason great pianists revel in recording, or playing live, the cycle of his thirty-two piano sonatas. Nearly every sonata tells a story from Beethoven's life, culminating in the final notes of the closing piece which appear to accept both death and salvation. Edward Sackville-West described the end of Opus 111 as "depositing us gently on the edge of eternity."

At the close of sonata 32, in the final moment of his widely-hailed cycle in London, Barenboim quietly pushed his chair under the piano, then prayerfully shut the piano's lid. Grown men, it is said, wept. Martin Kettle observed in *The Guardian*: "There are few things I know with any confidence. One is that, in these piano sonatas, Beethoven went further towards expressing the vast scope of the human spirit in sound than anyone before or since." Michael Henderson in *The Telegraph* went further, calling Beethoven "possibly the most protean spirit in the history of human endeavor. To tire of his music is to renounce life itself."

Having spent my 60th birthday with Beethoven, I

was determined to do the same for my 25th wedding anniversary a little more than two months later. It would turn out to be a memorable evening, and no wonder: the fabled Alban Berg Quartet's farewell New York performance, featuring Haydn, Berg and, of course, Beethoven, with opus 132 offering my first live experience of the *Heiliger Dankgesang.* The playing was, maybe, a little creaky but the emotion, at least in my seat, was profound.

On the same evening, a few dozen miles to the north and east, at his home in Stamford, Conn., iconic conservative author/columnist William F. Buckley was discussing with a pianist friend, Larry Perelman, the latter's performance of Beethoven's *Diabelli Variations* set for the following night. Perelman, a Soviet émigré, had long played privately for the writer, his family and friends (including young editors at Buckley-founded *National Review*), paying him back for his support for Soviet Jews over the years. Buckley had written about his love for classical music on many occasions, and Perelman often played for him some of Beethoven's piano sonatas, such as *The Tempest.*

Buckley once observed, "Life can't be all bad when for ten dollars you can buy all the Beethoven sonatas and listen to them for ten years."

On this night, the 82-year-old writer appeared under the weather but as usual was in hearty spirits, enjoying a few drinks before and during dinner, as the two men agreed that the pianist would skip some of the repeated passages in the *Variations* to keep the recital under an hour. Then Perelman helped his host, who was suffering from emphysema, to an early bedtime, but only after Buckley listened to his favorite piece of music, Beethoven's Piano Concerto No. 4.

The next morning, we would learn that William F. Buckley, after his night of Beethoven, had died. After reading pianist Perelman's account of his final night on the *National Review* site, I posted on my blog, from YouTube, Helene Grimaud playing the second movement of Buckley's beloved Piano Concerto No. 4. After all of these decades, I had finally found common ground with Mr. Conservative.

CHAPTER NINE

Playing Beethoven: The Trombonist

A number of famous artists live in my village, including Jonathan Demme, Bill Irwin, and Ellen Burstyn (not to mention Rosie O'Donnell), but Joseph Alessi is my new hometown hero. While pianists or violinists often get star turns out front, Alessi, as trombonist, stands or sits rather anonymously in the rear right of the New York Philharmonic orchestra, just part of a massive ensemble, and sometimes a rather small part of it. How does he relate to Beethoven's music, I wondered? What does Beethoven sound like back there, in the middle of the maelstrom? While you can often read the emotional gestures or grimaces of a solo or chamber performer from your seat, it's usually impossible to closely observe the orchestra players beyond the front ranks.

A few years back, as I've mentioned, I happened to coach Alessi's son in Little League. Joe sometimes showed up for games, and I don't recall knowing that he was even a musician, let alone a veteran with the New York Phil.   Not that this would have impressed me all that much at the time, still years away from my Beethoven obsession.   One thing's for certain: I'd never seen him perform.

That changed a few years later, although in a tragic context.   One of the kids on that same Little League team with Joe's son was Stephen Albert, a personal favorite who would star on my squads for several years.   His dad, Jon Albert, was passionate about baseball, and ended up coaching with me most of those years.   One night in September 2011, Jon called me to discuss some troubling Little League matters (he was on the local board while coaching with me in "fall ball").   The next day he perished in the attack on the World Trade Center. He had worked on one of the highest floors.   Several weeks later, when his widow, Donna, finally abandoned hope that her husband had survived, she held a local tribute for him.   I spoke.   Joe Alessi brought along several Philharmonic colleagues and played.

I hadn't seen him since – except in the back of the orchestra on stage – but he readily agreed to sit for an interview at his home.

Alessi's father, it turns out, played trumpet in the Metropolitan Opera orchestra and his mother sang in the chorus there.   They later moved to San Rafael, California, and Joe was playing with the San Francisco Ballet Orchestra by the age of sixteen. Then he attended the Curtis Institute of Music in Philadelphia, and five years later, in 1985, was hired as "principal trombone" at the NY Phil.   He has since cut several albums, performed with his own ensemble, and now teaches at Julliard and in his own Alessi Seminar series.

When I asked about his earliest "relationship" with Beethoven, I was surprised to learn just how little the composer wrote for the trombone – though, as with so many other things, he still managed to break new ground. "There's not much to practicing with Beethoven," Alessi explained. "He didn't really write that much for the instrument — nothing except in the 5th, 6th and 9th symphonies, part of the *Missa Solemnis* and *Fidelio*, maybe an overture, no chamber pieces at all." To that point in history, the trombone was pretty much only used with choral pieces, such as in Mozart's masses, Haydn's *The Creation*, and so forth. The sound from the three sizes of trombone happens to match the timbre of alto, tenor and bass voices, Alessi explained.

Growing up he'd "listen to records but only on how the trombone fit into the orchestra," Alessi said. "So my relationship with Beethoven really came later from my position in the orchestra," he added, "and with many different conductors, such as playing the Ninth live on TV with Zubin Mehta in Central Park for the anniversary of the Statue of Liberty. I did miss playing the Ninth with Lenny [Bernstein] in Germany when the Berlin Wall came down.

"My son had more experience with Beethoven at an early age, playing piano—we'd get videos on *The Story of Beethoven* and so on." In fact, his son, also named Joseph, first got into Beethoven, and music, via the *Pastoral* section of Disney's *Fantasia*, not an uncommon initiation back then.

Even in the pieces Beethoven wrote that included trombone, Alessi usually doesn't enter until well into the piece. This is known as a "long sit" for the musician, and even then, he or she often plays for only a few moments. Alessi put it this way: "The trombonist is only used as a field-goal kicker: You stand on the sidelines for a long time and then when you appear it's in a high-pressure situation. That's the life of the trombone player!" Until he's called on "the challenge is to sit up straight, not nod off. Of course, you can listen to the great music and watch the conductor.

"But when we do come in it's usually something difficult. It's very exposed. You have to be perfect. If you miss something you feel bad. You've sat there and done nothing and everyone else is working hard, so when you come in you want to be perfect. If a violinist misses one note it's not a big deal because they play thousands. Our ratio of notes is much lower. If we miss something everyone's going to hear it."

Surely the most famous trombone passage in all of music is the opening fanfare of the final movement of the Fifth Symphony, not just for the power and the drama but as the first use of the instrument in a symphony or in any other major piece without a choir. Alessi estimated he's played the Fifth maybe 120 times. I wondered how he prepared for that big movement in the nearly half-hour "sit" on stage.

"You're probably in a semi-comatose state," he revealed with a chuckle. "Everyone else is playing, especially the trumpet, and their instruments are warmer. Our instruments are cold, so the pitch has changed. We need to bring the instruments up to playing pitch, so we start blowing silently through the instruments, to get the temperature correct. If we come in on a cold instrument we will be flatter than anyone else. It also gets your body going. Then you empty out the condensation in the instrument, moisten your chops, and make sure your slide is unlocked — forgetting that has happened to many trombone players! Very comical.

"Then start watching the conductor, breathe, and make your entrance. For trombone players a lot of our success is to be awake, alert — and make your entrance on time."

But after 120 times, and probably at least twice every season, can the Fifth still be exciting for him? "Yeah, it's a fun part, and very challenging," he replied. "I play the part on alto. There are a couple of notes you have to pick out of there that are a bit difficult, such as a high F." I'd read somewhere that this was the highest note ever written for the instrument. "If you miss that everyone is going to hear you missed it. And at the very end of the symphony there's a high E. If you miss that, same thing. You really can't hide. It's a major league thing. If you don't have the high chops then it's a disaster.

"I'm never bored listening to it, that's for sure. Playing it is always an event. Everyone has their own version. Mainly the tempo distinguishes one from another."

What about the Sixth Symphony? Technically, this was actually the first use of the trombone for a symphony since it was written just ahead of the Fifth, though given a later opus number. Again, Alessi explained, it's "very limited-- even worse, a longer sit." The first entrance is during the loud, incredibly dynamic, storm movement. "BAHHHH — just one note," he said, making the sound. "Some nice, longer notes later. A supporting role, but some touchy things—again, if you miss anything, people are going to hear you. You're a bit naked."

And the Ninth? He's played it about eighty times, he guesses, with Kurt Masur's version perhaps the most memorable, because of the conductor's passion for it. "I believe in the 3rd movement, the *adagio*, there are a few bars for trombone," he said. "Then you stop and put your horn down for another 20 minutes. I don't even know why he wrote that part in the *adagio*. Maybe to keep us awake. Or maybe the trombone players weren't that good back then.

"Then, after a twenty minute wait, you come in with something very difficult. Very exposed. Very high. We get our wake-up call. Man, if you miss anything it's a disaster. Then after the 'Ode to Joy,' the bass trombone player comes in, the bass choir comes in with it. Then I play a lot, very intense." One trombone passage accompanies the choir singing:

> *You millions, I embrace you.*
> *This kiss is for all the world!*
> *Brothers, above the starry canopy*
> *There must dwell a loving Father.*

So what did he feel, way in the back, while playing Beethoven? "It's funny," he replied, "I never listen to Beethoven in an emotional way. I don't know why. Brahms hits me, or Prokofiev. Their melodies are just so lush. The finale of the Ninth: I'm certainly enjoying the music. There may be an alto or tenor singing right in my ear! It's the sound I'm captivated by, wallowing in the sound. Of course by this time Beethoven wasn't hearing at all. The fact he composed this whole thing, I don't know how he did it.

"There are many pieces I could live without playing again, though none from Beethoven. There are many modern day pieces that are horrible, I can't believe we are playing them in the first place. But it's very subjective. Something the musicians don't like playing the audience could love."

Alessi has played Beethoven all over the world. I wondered how audiences abroad respond differently. He admitted he was "more nervous playing those pieces in Europe, because there's such a great tradition there, and people there tend to know more about music. They are more educated in the classics and their own music. All those composers composed their stuff there, they're like national heroes." He visited the graves of Beethoven and Brahms in Vienna.

But are audiences younger there? He wasn't sure. "Over here, it's almost dying," he observed. "A lot of senior citizens coming to our concerts; at one point they were young people listening to rock and roll. But long ago, you got some introduction to composers in school. Now? Today, the average young person has probably never heard Beethoven, ever, or just a passage here and there in a movie or on TV without even knowing who wrote it."

Suddenly Alessi recalled that Beethoven had written one chamber piece for trombones, called the *Equali*, apparently for a funeral. It's in four very short movements for four trombones and Joe was actually one of the few to record it with his own group. Though rarely played, he observed, "It's definitely Beethovenian, you know that he wrote it."

Alessi took out his laptop and searched for some background. It turns out that the piece was played at one of the most famous funerals in history, Beethoven's own. At a trombone history site we found one account: "By the morning of 26 March 1827, not a doubt remained that the impending loss [Beethoven's death] was all too near. Mr. Haslinger went to Mr. Kapellmeister von Seyfried to discuss the possibility of forming a choral anthem out of these *Equali* to the words of the *Miserere*, and thus to escort the mortal remains of our prince of composers to eternal peace to the mournful sounds of his own creations. ..."

In closing, I asked Alessi if there were any other minor Beethoven pieces he got to play away from the Philharmonic. "I like some of the string quartets," he said, "and, of course, trombone players will make arrangements of string quartets or trios, and I have a bunch of arrangements at home. So if a trombone player comes over here and he says, 'Let's play some Beethoven' — we're all set!"

CHAPTER TEN

Obey Thoven

In the years since my Beethovenmania first struck, the obsession has ebbed only a little. I've attended dozens of concerts since, downloaded hundreds of movements or entire pieces, viewed countless videos, read another nine or ten books. Beyond that, I saw Jane Fonda on Broadway in *33 Variations*, written by Moises Kaufman, which portrayed Beethoven's struggle to write the *Diabelli Variations*. I caught Stephen Dillane's off-Broadway performance of T.S. Eliot's "Four Quartets," paired with the Miro Quartet playing the work that inspired it, Beethoven's opus 132, including the *Heiliger Dankgesang*. (Kate Winslet was there, too.)

When Dudamel made his debut with the Los Angeles Philharmonic, conducting the Ninth, I witnessed it live online. I watched the young Polish pianist Piotr Andrewsjewski in concert and later when he took questions after a screening of a film about him. When I attended my first "Mostly Mozart" concert at Lincoln Center (for a Beethoven piece, naturally), I sat right on stage behind the orchestra, for a pair of Beethoven pieces. I viewed an acclaimed new film about Glenn Gould and became friends with classical music writer Tim Page, who recounted some of his endless middle-of-the-night phone calls from Gould.

Taking the opportunity to ask a true expert this question, I put it to Tim Page: "Maybe I am, in my ignorance, going a bit bananas over Beethoven. Perhaps he is he not as truly great as all that?" Page replied with this immortal line: "It's *impossible* to overrate Beethoven."

Despite the evidence of Beethoven, I still did not necessarily believe in god, but that failed to keep me from attending performances of the *C Major Mass* in two Westchester churches, and the *Missa Solemnis* twice at Avery Fisher Hall. And on Twitter, my "Sunday Morning in the Church of Beethoven" feature (with a link to a different YouTube video every week) drew a wide following. Also via Twitter I got to ask former New York Philharmonic conductor Loren Maazel to name his favorite movement from Beethoven. Surprisingly, for an orchestra leader, he picked the slow movement of the master's *Spring* violin sonata. Also via Twitter, I talked Beethoven with everyone from youngish folk-rocker Joseph Arthur to longtime favorite Rosanne Cash.

I even read Rita Dove's book-length narrative poem, *Sonata Mulattica*, which tells the more-or-less true story of half-black violinist George Bridgewater, who travels to Vienna and becomes friendly with Beethoven. Ludwig writes a sonata in his honor but takes away the dedication to the musician when Bridgewater fancies the same woman. In one of the lyrical interludes, Beethoven himself speaks:

I am by nature a conflagration;
I would rather leap
Than sit and be looked at.

My appetite for checking Google News for daily Beethoven references hardly waned. R. Kelly, it seems, donned a tuxedo during several of his U.S. concerts to conduct a recording of Beethoven's Fifth Symphony. An artist named Sara Naim had concocted a fascinating experiment photographing milk while subjecting it to sounds waves from the *Moonlight* sonata, resulting in vibratory snapshots. Bizarrely, one of the companies that produce baseball cards had embedded a strand of Beethoven's hair in one card as some kind of sales promotion. This combined two of my favorite things in the world – Beethoven and baseball – but hardly seemed dignified. Over in the UK, a recently discovered six-word shopping list, in Beethoven's hand, had sold for some 49,000 pounds.

Meanwhile, I was delighted to find that the two key scenes at the finish of *The King's Speech*, winner of the Academy Award for Best Picture in 2011, had as their soundtrack long excerpts from LvB's 7th Symphony and Piano Concerto No. 5. My wife bought for me from eBay a Beethoven "action figure," although all the plastic Ludwig really does is swing his arms, perhaps angry at his assistant

Schindler or a hapless musician.   Later she gave me a Beethoven finger puppet.

In the fall of 2011, classical station WQXR in New York City launched its biggest promotion ever. They called it, as an inside joke, "Beethoven Awareness Month," knowing he was fairly well-known to begin with. Posters appeared all over the city with Ludwig's image and OBEY THOVEN, a tribute by one famous street artist (Shepard Fairey) to another (Banksy). A WQXR spokesman said they were even considering producing mugs and t-shirts emblazoned with: "Beethoven was Def." They sponsored concerts and other events for an entire month, and even passed out Beethoven "tattoos" at Grand Central Terminal.   A friend managed to obtain three of the tattoos and gave them to me but again the question emerged: What would Beethoven say?

YouTube provided a never-ending trove of curiosities.   If I wanted to compare 37 different versions of the final moments of the Ninth (which conductors rushed it?), I could do so (and I did). Another video presented the hallowed solo opening of Piano Concerto No. 4 as played by ten famous pianists.

The concert trail had now taken me to the newly renovated Alice Tully and Zankel halls in New York, plus out-of-town venues I'd only read about previously in *New York Times* or *New Yorker* listings: Music Mountain and Norfolk in Connecticut, Marlboro in Vermont, Caramoor in Westchester County, plus a fine weekly series at my hometown Nyack Library.   There were weekend concerts at what's known as Bargemusic, on an actual converted barge docked almost directly under the Brooklyn Bridge. We've returned to Tanglewood a half dozen times. When we saw the Ninth for the second time there we sat in the second row center. Later I caught the Ninth in a church, at Philharmonic Hall, and at the largest cathedral in the West, St. John the Divine in New York.

I finally plunged deeply into the string quartets (beyond the *Heiliger Dankgesang*), loving the mid-period "Razumovsky" set of three and the *Harp* nearly as much as the fabled late quartets. I caught more than a dozen different quartets live, with Pacifica a favorite (and Takacs getting the nod on recordings). Similarly, I fully embraced the late piano sonatas, with Michiko Uchida traversing all three at Carnegie especially memorable. She played them one after another, requesting no applause in-between, feeling they were of a piece. As the poet Robert Browning wrote: "The grandeur of Beethoven's thirty-second piano sonata represents the opening of the gates of heaven."

Uchida also provided another highlight. At Marlboro the renowned summer session traditionally ends with Beethoven's *Choral Fantasia*, a completely wonderful (if not beloved by all critics) 18-minute piece that opens as a piano sonata, then turns into a piano concerto, before closing with a chorus. The melody strongly prefigures the "Ode to Joy." The two directors of the summer program, Richard Goode and Uchida, perform it in alternate summers. We happened to get Uchida and I'll never forget the unabashed delight on her face as she looked up from her piano at the young people she had mentored, now playing and singing so well. I was afraid that at any moment she would forget her parts to race over and hug someone.

It could have gone on forever as far as I was concerned. The conductor, we later learned, was Ignat Solzhenitzen, middle son of the Russian author. Alex Ross of *The New Yorker* sang in the choir.

About this time, I came across the blog Think Denk, written by up-and-coming New York pianist Jeremy Denk He didn't blog often but when he did the results were often hilarious takes on touring mishaps or, in his most famous entry, an imagined conversation with Sarah Palin about, among other things, Beethoven. He could have called it "Going Fugue."

Oddly, his "interview" with Palin helped draw me into the *Hammerklavier* at last. Denk asked her about that piece, and she replied: "Well, ya know, Beethoven was the dude who said thanks but no thanks to Napoleon. Plus from all the mavericky songs he wrote, maybe this one could be known as the most maverickyest." Also she had allegedly titled a college thesis *Trickle-Down Fugonomics: A Reaganian Model of Beethoven's Counterpoint* — and now explained, "That's how I got funding from the American Enterprise Institute."

And Sarah on the *Hammerklavier's* massive slow movement: "I gotta confess, I usually fast forward through that one…. It's kind of a bummer. And since unlike some Americans out there I don't hate America, I don't want to dwell on all that negativity….I mean didn't he already write the *Archduke* trio, which is ALSO in B-flat major? Why couldn't he just write the trio again? I know a lotta

folks out there, in Main Street all across this land of
ours, they'll tell you, they're just more *Archduke*
kinda folks then they are *Hammerklavier* folks."

Asked for advice as he set out to perform the
Hammerklavier around the country, Palin replied,
"Trill, baby, trill!"

Subsequently, I grew absorbed in the piece's slow
movement, which reaches depths of scary (and
scared) emotion that only the final sonatas approach.
So it was great to watch Denk nail it live at Zankel.
A year later I heard his rendering of sonata no. 32 in
a late-Saturday night program at Lincoln Center, the
best performance of it I'd seen live.

Surely one of highlights of this Era of Beethoven
was a trip to London (my first in thirty years) with
my wife, where we caught three Beethoven concerts
plus a rehearsal at St. Martin's in the Fields within six
days. Oh, we also managed to squeeze in my
daughter's wedding while we were there.

Well, that's quite a bit misleading. The wedding
invite came first, and certainly took priority, but then
I checked online to see if we could fit in a little
Ludwig. So we enjoyed the *Pastoral* symphony in a
church and two chamber performances at Wigmore
Hall. Yes, we also attended the wedding rehearsal
dinner, the wedding itself and the gala reception (in
a famous Fleet Street pub), and met my daughter for
lunch and dinner on other days. What a week!

Too bad we missed what must have been, on
some level, the performance of the year: the eight-
member Ukulele Orchestra of Great Britain at
London's annual Proms strumming bits of the Ninth,
accompanied by a thousand other uke players in the
audience.

On the other hand, nothing could keep me away from a New York Philharmonic concert in Central Park, kicking off their annual summer tour of the boroughs. They would close with Beethoven's Symphony No. 7. I had only been to one other Phil in the Park performance ever. It took place in the 1970s and it must have included the *1812 Overture*, because I recall cannons going off. Now we arrived hours before the evening event on a spotless summer day expecting to sit near the stage but finding that several thousand got there ahead of us. Still, we ended up with good "seats" (on the ground), as a mammoth crowd filled in behind us, covering the lawn with more than 100,000 bodies. Rain held off until, literally, the final note.

In a piece for Huffington Post, I would dub it "Ludwigstock." But no one stripped naked or dropped brown acid (although clouds of pot occasionally drifted through). The crowd was filled with parents and grandparents and kids from two to twenty. Most amazing: During the famous funeral march, you could — I know this is hard to believe — almost hear a pin drop. Even the babies stopped crying. It was so quiet you could hear the automobile traffic in the distance on Fifth Avenue or Central Park West. That's called "holding an audience." Surely this was one of the greatest silent tributes ever offered a composer — or anyone.

A quite different tribute, involving an even larger assembly, arrived on October 15, 2011. That day had been set as a global day of protest, drawing on the burgeoning Occupy movement, labor unions, students and anti-austerity activists, among others. The biggest turnout materialized in Madrid, with a crowd estimated at perhaps half a million gathering in the Puerta del Sol after dark. From afar it was hard to judge all that happened that evening, but videos that I found on YouTube a few hours after the event suggested that the high point might have been a performance of part of the fourth movement of the Ninth Symphony — the "Ode to Joy" segment and then the finale — by a small, ragtag, amateur orchestra. While the sound of Beethoven was small, it was amplified out to the massive audience in the famous square.

Videos captured it from numerous angles. Astounding was an elevated shot that showed the entirety of the crowd, as the hundreds of thousands erupted as one at the close. Even more affecting: a camera from just behind the orchestra found the local Dudamel conducting the mere handful of musicians as young dancers on a platform moved in ecstasy. Many near the orchestra wept openly, before exploding in screams and chants (vowing peaceful resistance) when it was over. Never in my experience was the image of Beethoven as the "universal composer" more moving, and undeniable.

CHAPTER ELEVEN

Playing Beethoven: The Pianist

After attending maybe fifty Beethoven concerts in three years, and reading hundreds of thousands of words about musicians and their views of the composer, I hungered to chat with some of them myself about life with Ludwig. Two candidates presented themselves immediately.

One, as we've seen, was Joseph Alessi. The other was Jeremy Denk, now 41, who in just a few years had leaped from little known to possibly the hottest pianist in New York. When New York's WQXR, in November 2011, held an all-day marathon with more than a dozen pianists, (including top younger players such as Jonathan Biss) performing all 32 of Beethoven's sonatas, they chose Denk to do the *Hammerklavier* and then close it all with the Opus 111. Naturally, I was there.

As I've noted, my introduction to Jeremy came via his viral "interview" with Sarah Palin back in 2008. Now, when I contacted him via email, he agreed to sit down with me to talk Beethoven over lunch, even though he was in the middle of his usual hectic concertizing. Having just performed the unlikely and difficult pairing of Ives' *Concord* sonata and Bach's *Goldberg Variations*, he had suddenly flown to Los Angeles to fill in for an ill pianist on Beethoven's Piano Concerto #1, conducted by Dudamel. All the while practicing for numerous upcoming recitals.

Denk's blog continued to offer plenty of wise or funny Beethoven references as well. He's also written a pair of pieces for *The New Yorker* in the past year.

There is probably a better way of putting this. But who cares? I enjoy Beethoven the most when he doesn't insist so much on being "manly." For example, the Eroica Symphony is just manly enough; the last movement of the Fifth Symphony is way too manly, etcetera..

He's a trickster, an unreliable narrator, willing to whip out the rug out from under you, scheming behind your back how to mislead you next. This fascinating willingness even to disrespect his own beautiful inspirations, to destroy moods he has carefully created: a neglected ingredient of Beethoven's Greatness.

It struck me that one of the recurring, characteristic, marvelous gestures of the 4th Concerto is this: sending a note up, to see what will happen to it. Notes are left, for periods of time, to fend for themselves. This is very different from arranging your notes' flights first, reserving hotels, etc. Luckily the notes of the 4th Concerto know what do with their free time. Put another way, the notes of the 4th might need a manager, but get by with inspiration and beauty, like so many people on Earth.

Denk, raised in New Mexico, went on to study music at Oberlin and at Indiana University, before beginning the slow climb to fame in New York City. He is notable not only for the precision of his playing but also for his daring programs and partnerships. Denk often performs with crowd favorite Joshua Bell but also sits in with little-known ensembles, and it seemed like he would play anything, from Bach to Ives and Ligeti and beyond.

We met at an eatery near his apartment on the Upper West Side and the following ensued. I was relieved that he arrived on time, as he had warned on his blog that he can't figure out why he can remember every note of the *Goldberg Variations* but can easily forget his room number in a hotel.

Tell me about growing up with Beethoven – were you a fan early on or was it more like eat-your-peas?

I definitely have a lot of complicated childhood memories playing Beethoven. I wasn't nearly as in love with Beethoven as I was, say, Mozart or Brahms as a kid. I don't know why. Every audition you are ever going to play they were going to judge you playing Beethoven — Mozart is "too easy."

I remember when I was 13, 14, trying my hand at the *Waldstein* sonata and I was pretty miserable about it, but now I just adore that piece, it's very redemptive and wonderful. It was a misery then. The *Waldstein* then had things that I wasn't able to do, therefore it was frustrating. I didn't think of it as a piece I would ever play. Then I played it again in my mid-30s. There are so many miraculous things about that piece that you don't recognize as a kid, obviously.

Why did you do a double major, with chemistry, at Oberlin?

My parents were a little nervous about...music. "Tinkling the keys."

At Oberlin I worked a lot on the *Appassionata*, which I found difficult and terrifying. I simply couldn't work my way through those problems. Also I didn't have a tremendous identification with the music itself, perhaps because I found it so well-trodden. People using it as a judgment on whether you can play piano or not does not exactly excite the creative juices.

Also, I didn't identify much in those days with Beethoven's middle period, the "heroic" style. Now the *Archduke* trio is perhaps my very favorite piece in the world to play. When I went to Bloomington, my teacher there, when he spoke about Beethoven, offered a fresh look at the dead white Europeans. Before then Beethoven for me represented a certain smoothness, the recordings were in the tradition of everything subdivided perfectly – even today that is not one of my interpretive aims, that "epic smoothness." I feel a certain antipathy to that.

Once my teacher was coaching us on the *Archduke* and he said it was "the only truly beautiful thing ever written for the piano." It's true that in that slow movement Beethoven achieves something about the way the piano sounds that was so perfect.

I worked on the *Eroica* variations a lot as a student, played that a lot in competition. I loved playing the final cello sonata, that crazy fugue. The more outlandish Beethoven was the more I liked him. I worked a lot on opus 109 but I didn't play opus 111 [the final sonata] until almost the age of 30. Towards the end Beethoven became much more obsessed with the story-telling element of music. The number of movements in each piece was changed to fit the story. So he was not constrained – that's incredibly appealing to me. Rather than become obsessed by his tragic life story, I get into his throwing off of constraints and the story telling.

What do you think of the claim you shouldn't play those late sonatas when young – supposedly not ready for the profundity?

I kind of, basically, subscribe to that. I'm sure I will have a very different perspective when I'm in my 50s. But I'm really attracted to them as everyone is. They're so instantly beautiful. They seem to promise so much.

Why? What is so profound about them?

Each of the last three have their own message to impart. Number 111 is the one I've spent the most time thinking about and have the most "mature" perspective on it. I've never played 110 because I've heard it so often in auditions it drives me out of my mind — people feel there's a sweetness in it that they want to bring out and actually that piece also has something much stronger, more earthshaking. So I've been avoiding it.

But 111 is a piece I can't leave behind. For one thing, he is revisiting all of his C-minor work — after all the *sturm and drang*, he's coming back and sweeping all these old ideas into this. Everything in the first movement is about an onrushing, and then all these little moments of trying to stop. And that's a very profound life statement that maybe young people are not quite so well attuned to, you know what I mean? Desperate attempts to extract repose from this onrush. Then those little stoppages explode into this endless C- minor river. And the way that river responds to the mini-stoppages, and then erases all memory of that.

By then Beethoven was more and more concerned with the notion of returning after complete disintegration. And that's not something you may recognize at certain times in your life, you don't get all the resonances. You don't feel as incredibly torn by it. I didn't get that at the beginning but now it's one of those weirdly supercharged pieces for me — the most difficult to get through without becoming emotional myself.

What are you feeling up there on stage while playing?

You have to distinguish between musical feeling and personal feeling. They have strong connections, obviously. In the case of the 2nd movement of 111, you have embarked on this thing and there's a sense of getting lost in the contemplation of this thing, chromatically everything dissolves, and there's this sense of complete lostness. It's a very musical feeling in one sense but held very tightly to a certain experience of life that's very familiar.

But it's a way the music seems to represent something so profound. When it returns at the end that is the moment I become overwhelmed. But in a sense it's written to be overwhelming – the way it emerges, and gathers – he was getting better and better at that. Beethoven in 111 is representing a profound sense of heaven, maybe connected to the Buddhist idea of nirvana where you relinquish everything after a lifetime of struggle.

A lot of the middle period stuff is about waves, harmonies. In the late stuff he uses those waves for different purposes. And the return at the end of 111 —I think he was thinking about the *Goldberg Variations* when he was writing, the return of the theme and simplicity after incredible complexity. It's a very musical thing on one hand, but it's also a thing about life that music is particularly well-suited for. Does that make any sense?

Ever think of Beethoven's life story when performing?

I confess I have not studied Beethoven's bio very much. I'm a little averse to biographies, even of authors I like, such as Proust. I know with the last sonatas he had accepted what had happened to his life and that he had decided to do something that no one had ever done before, and not to give up.

Beethoven happened to have a great story—a publicist's dream!

You seem inspired by Beethoven's humor and playfulness.

Even 111 has a certain humor in the last movement, which is folded into the general joy of playing it. I love Beethoven when he is being funny, which is why I enjoyed playing the *Eroica* variations.

That's a problem of mine with classical music in general and not just Beethoven: Looking around the concert hall when there's something funny going on and seeing everyone so serious. That's a real disconnect for me in the classical music experience — humor and play, without trivializing the profundity of the music. And that's one of the really great Beethoven artistic achievements, this kind of making even the most profound works also the most ridiculous in some way. Like with the *Hammerklavier*, the *scherzo*, even parts of the fugue, it's the absurdly funny and crazy folded into the most heaven-shaking.

The romantics didn't get that — like with Wagner, everything had to be profound.

What can you guess about Beethoven as a pianist?

He had an amazing left hand, he wrote incredibly difficult for the left hand, equally as hard for the right hand. He was a pianist through and through, he understood the colors of the piano. The late sonatas had brand new overtones.

What about trill, baby, trill?

He became incredibly obsessed with trills late in his life. I'm sure he had extraordinary technique but at a certain point I'm sure he didn't really care. His famous trills I think are difficult for everyone. It depends on the piano. I played 111 in Denver a couple of months ago and I thought one of the trills was a disaster. And I'd practiced that trill to within an inch of my life and some of the other ones too!

Some people get obsessed with how many "trill wiggles" so-and-so played. I've never been a big trill wiggler counter. But I love the way his trills pass over into a different sound. Obviously he got so obsessed with them.

Are you a big fan of Beethoven's non-piano music?

Yes I am, although obviously much less attuned to them. I still have religious experiences listening to some of them. The Razumovsky quartets, for some reason, I am nuts about. They are as great as the late quartets. I hear a lot of Beethoven symphonies, because I am in the hall, backstage after I perform.

Have you listened to Liszt's piano transcriptions of the symphonies?

No, just here and there. It seems a little greedy—we have these 32 piano sonatas and more. Probably some reviewers would say, why would you play these, you can listen to the symphonies, what do they bring? They are pretty faithful adaptations.

What about your feelings about the Ninth?

Honestly, I haven't heard that piece in a long time, 20 years at least. It's weird. I used to listen to it obsessively as a kid. When I was 12 it was completely my obsession. I had three different recordings of it. Now I don't hear it because piano music is never played before it — it's a stand alone event, almost as much a happening as a symphony.

It's impossible to talk about that piece, which is also true of the *Goldberg Variations*. I don't have enough *chutzpah* to talk about them. So much baggage has been piled on them one way or another, they're like celebrities, you know what I mean? What is there left to say? It's a thrilling experience, the Ninth as a whole.

Do you see it connected to his late piano pieces?

There are a lot of connections between that and what he's doing in the late piano and late quartets. The first three movements of the Ninth seems to fit in the late style but the last movement is sort of an aberration, and it's not what he was doing otherwise. It's wild, though, but a different kind of wild.

I wish I had some searing insights about it now, like I'm sure I had when I was 12.... There's something proto-minimalist about the piece, that's what strikes me some times.

Mitsuko Uchida says playing the late piano sonatas changed the way she will play piano from now on. Makes sense to you?

Sure, yeah, there are certain composers who point out your weaknesses. I felt that when playing the *Hammerklavier.* The most terrifying things technically, you just have to look them in the eye and say, this has to be done, to find a solution. It would show you something physically about your playing that might change you after, some connection that was not happening. In order to play at that level it causes you to search.

Each composer has certain musical grammar. I used to be so insecure about Beethoven but now I feel at home with that language for some reason, weirdly. But it's true you do change your technique depending on who you play. I find it with Bach. With some composers you can be more lazy.

I liked your comment about preferring Beethoven when he's not so "manly."

That's for sure. Consequently I am ambivalent about a key element of Beethoven's style, that heroic style. I don't like the violin concerto that much. The 7th symphony if not played really well can be a little tiresome. The final movement of the Fifth Symphony.

Beethoven, who (shall we say) had many flaws as a person seemed to feel his only chance to get to heaven was writing these incredible pieces.

He thought it was his destiny. I think Schubert thought that too. You don't think Beethoven thought he was a god in his own right?

Partly, but I'd also say he saw his composing as his only ticket to heaven.

The whole message of the last piano sonatas is

incredibly religious in that sense, complete surrender to the greater good, far away from the normal. You know he felt that way, when you read about him. It wasn't just absolute music to him, he was also always thinking about spiritual messages.

Now you've made me pensive about Beethoven.

APPENDIX

Beethoven on Film

By Greg Mitchell

As noted earlier in this book, Beethoven has been the subject of numerous film features and documentaries since the silent era, few of them completely satisfactory (*Immortal Beloved* and *Copying Beethoven* the most recent examples) and some bizarre, almost laughable.

One of the first films I came across on DVD was the terrific BBC film from 2003 titled *Eroica*, which portrayed the first rehearsal of the symphony in 1804 at the palace of patron Prince Lobkowitz (yes, this happened). It stars as Beethoven a headstrong Ian Hart, who had earlier played on film — and was dead ringer for — John Lennon. (In *Eroica*, I expected him to burst into "Roll Over, Beethoven," at any moment). Frank Finlay portrays a skeptical

Haydn, who comes a-calling midway through the
rehearsal, and proclaims at the end — borrowing
from what he actually said at the public premiere —
"From today, everything is different." Haydn also
says in the film that Beethoven had done "something
remarkable," for the first time putting the composer
at the "center of the work."

During the rehearsal we see a fiery Beethoven
claim he is the equal of any nobleman and he directly
takes on a hostile Tim Pigott-Smith as a snooty
military officer. He hangs out with the "common"
musicians, and defends Napoleon as a populist,
while barely tolerating the prince. John Gardiner's
orchestra, properly playing period instruments,
closes with a smashing fourth movement, earning
approval from Haydn. Celebrating at a bar, Ludwig
hears that Napoleon has declared himself emperor –
and then scratches out the dedication to him on his
score (this also happened, though probably not in a
pub). At the end he walks home with his assistant
Ries, making the first reference in the film to losing
his hearing.

Thanks to YouTube – more and more, a key
Beethoven delivery system for me – I was able to
watch snatches of many other film treatments, even
entire movies. There are even animated Beethoven
shorts for kids. Still, I didn't care enough to watch
any of the Beethoven-the-dog films (culminating in,
naturally, *Beethoven's Fifth*) to find out why the mutt
was named after the composer.

The earliest film on record seems to be an
Austrian silent, *Der Martyrer Seines Herzens* ("The
Martyr of the Heart"), directed by Emil Justiz in 1918,
with Frutz Kortner as Beethoven. Also appearing

that year : *La dixième symphonie* ("The 10th Symphony") by the great Abel Gance, one of film's most innovative creators. This film, according to summaries, features a young girl, a murder, and blackmail. The girl later marries a composer who is a great admirer of Beethoven, but he eventually discovers her sordid past. He writes what he calls the 10th symphony, and labels it this way: " At the feet of his master Beethoven , a musician distraught by the treason of women, tries to forget and express his sadness."

Beethoven's Moonlight Sonata was made by James A. FitzPatrick (best known for travelogues) around 1920 for the Bell and Howell Company, and I watched the three-minute black and white short, tinted, online. It portrayed the mythic inspiration for the sonata (which Beethoven, in fact, never did label "Moonlight"). We see Ludwig and a friend walking under moonlight, when they hear piano music coming from a nearby cottage — a good trick for Beethoven, since he was already going deaf. Beethoven stops. He overhears a conversation between the young female pianist (who is blind!) and her brother. The girl expresses a wish to watch Beethoven perform at a concert in Cologne, but her brother observes they scarcely have enough money to pay the rent. "I will play for her!" Beethoven announces to his friend and strides mightily into the cottage. Discovering she is blind, he extinguishes the candles and improvises by... moonlight. The final card reads: "Thus Beethoven's immortalized sonata."

Next I came upon *Un Grand Amour de Beethoven* by (again) Abel Gance and made in 1936. It starred Harry Baur, who had previously played Jean Valjean in a 1934 film. (Baur, who was Jewish, would be tortured and killed by the Nazi Gestapo a few years later.) Also notable: the young Jean-Louis Barrault as nephew Karl.

From the YouTube clips it was hard to doubt the serious intent, with an anguished (and corpulent) Beethoven battling his demons and deafness at every turn. Several of the potential "immortal beloveds" are portrayed as well. The depiction of Beethoven's hearing cutting in and out, or overcome by buzzing, is depicted with more art and accuracy than in later Hollywood depictions. A walk in the countryside inspires the *Pastoral* symphony, and then during a violent storm he sits at the piano—he is living inside a windmill, for some reason—and like a mad man composes the "Storm" section of the symphony.

And then there's this travesty: Beethoven arrives uninvited at the wedding of one of his would-be lovers, bribes the organist, gets behind the keys—and substitutes for the "Wedding March" his Funeral March from the *Eroica* symphony. So even Gance would not avoid outright fiction and melodrama, the latter hardly needed in any film about Beethoven. Still, the film sold enough tickets that Warner Bros. planned *The Life of Beethoven*, starring Paul Muni, but that never went before the cameras. An Austrian film titled *Eroica*, starring Ewald Balser as Beethoven – with future star Oskar Werner as nephew Karl — was released in 1951.

As I skipped around YouTube, catching parts of later films, I realized how poorly Beethoven has fared on film (with the exception of a documentary here and there and parts of Hollywood and BBC docudramas). Throwing caution to the winds, I started watching *Beethoven's Nephew* from 1988, even though I'd heard it was awful and was directed by former Warhol director (*Heat, Flesh*, et al) Paul Morrissey. Sure enough, it went wildly wrong right from the first seconds, when it announced matter-of-"factly" that Beethoven had died in a former monastery.

It didn't get much better from there on, despite appearances by the great Natalie Baye as Leonore (an older woman who beds nephew Karl), plus Jane Birkin as Karl's mother. The composer's deafness comes and goes and, like nearly every treatment, the premiere of the Ninth Symphony is packed with errors. Ludwig seems to fancy young men. Beethoven even admits to his nephew that he picked up an STD years earlier. Wolfgang Reichmann was mainly fine as Ludwig but Dietmar Printz as nephew Karl is nothing but an untalented pretty boy straight out of the old Warhol/Morrissey films (an IMDB reviewer called him "a 42nd Street hustler in 19th century drag"). Apparently the film was based on two French books, one a fake memoir by Karl and the other about Karl titled *The Nephew of Beethoven*.

More curiosities followed. The legendary Erich Von Stroheim portrayed Beethoven in the epic 1955 film *Napoleon* directed by Sacha Guitry. And, yes, Beethoven has even gotten the Disney treatment. A film released in theaters in 1961, airing on Disney's TV series the following year, carried the awful title, *The Magnificent Rebel*. It starred little known (and unrealistically handsome) Karl Boehm as Ludwig. As LvB sits in a café with a love interest, musicians start playing one of his tunes and he complains they are playing too slow. The film also portrays the legend of how the opening of the Fifth Symphony came to be – showing Ludwig's landlord rap-rap-rapping on his door. And so on. A few minutes are posted on YouTube, and now there's a DVD version.

In the children's department, I found a well-known entry, *Beethoven Lives Upstairs*, a 1992 production out of Canada, directed by David Devine with Neil Munro as the composer. "Based on a true story," it finds Ludwig, while writing the Ninth, boarding at the house owned by a family with a boy named Christoph. The father feels this is a great privilege but the boy views the new lodger as a madman, and follows him around trying to prove that he is "crazy." Ludwig is indeed a big pain. He flings food at waiters and throws a maid out after she tosses scraps of his symphony. Slowly the boy comes to appreciate both man and music, and tells people: "People like Mr. Beethoven make rules they don't follow." He even gives the composer an ear trumpet as a gift. Then there's this classic exchange (fit for *Saturday Night Live*):

Christoph: "*Why does he have to write another Symphony? He's already made a Fourth, a Fifth, a Sixth, a Seventh, and an Eighth!*"
Uncle Kurt: "*And this one will be his Ninth.*"
Christoph: "*I hope it's his last!*"

Well, the film is better than that, and I discovered that it was distributed widely abroad, won several awards, and was (or is) taught in many schools. It emerged as a CD, book and audio book. I love this line from one guide for parents: "Several scenes are geared toward pre-adolescents who will be intrigued by Beethoven's independent spirit." A nice way of putting it.

Also at You Tube, I found three or four lengthy documentaries or docudramas of varying quality. The BBC's three-part *The Genius of Beethoven* was better than most. LvB was played by Paul Rhys (who once played Theo Van Gogh). In a stirring scene, Beethoven at a party is challenged to an improvisation competition by a renowned visitor — this type of thing often happened, apparently. Beethoven, introduced as "the toast of Vienna, we know him, we love him," naturally destroys the visitor, driving him from the salon, and probably the country, as the woman pant.

Then there's this bit of trivia: The former piano prodigy played by Jack Nicholson in the classic 1970s film *Five Easy Pieces* is called Bobby Dupea in the film but in the credits his full name appears as Robert Eroica Dupea — and his brother was Carl Fidelio Dupea. Not that many probably noticed.

It should not go unnoted, however, that perhaps the most famous "Beethoven film" of all is Kubrick's *A Clockwork Orange*. Malcolm McDowell's Alex is obsessed with the composer, particularly his Ninth Symphony ("oh it was gorgeousness and gorgeosity made flesh"), which eventually is used by the authorities to "cure" him via the "Ludovico" technique. We even see a poster of "the old Ludwig Van" in his bedroom. WikiPedia has this summary of the ways the film differs from Anthony Burgess's book:

— "In the film, when the Cat Lady assaults Alex, she holds a small bust of Beethoven, while Alex holds a large sculpted penis. In the novel, Alex wields a bust of Beethoven during their fight, while the Cat Lady attempts to fight back with a walking stick."

— "Alex is conditioned against all music in the book, but in the film he is only averse to Beethoven's Ninth Symphony. "

I would probably be remiss if I did not at least mention the *Saturday Night Live* sketch with John Belushi as a fiery Beethoven. Some fans have dubbed it "Belushthoven. " It's readily available at YouTube. Also look for a Dudley Moore parody of Beethoven at the piano.

The wildest film of all was, sadly, almost unwatchable, and irritating when you *can* stand it. An Argentinian musician/composer/theorist named Mauricio Kagel, then 38, decided to make a movie in 1969 called *Ludwig Van*, an impressionistic (to be kind) work with no story, plot or bit of sense to it. We visit some of the places Beethoven lived or worked but what do we see? A bathtub filled with busts of the composer, for example, and walls papered with the scores of his music. There's a lot of walking around the streets of Vienna with the camera aimed at the shoes of the cameraman. Beethoven (I think) appears in drag. Occasionally there is a moment or two of interesting speculation on his physical capacities, his skill, or what he wrote in his notebooks. The film, ends at a ...zoo. An elephant defecates to the chorus of the Ninth. The actual thud you heard, more likely, was Beethoven rolling over in his grave.

An interview with David Levy

David Benjamin Levy has taught in the music departments at Wake Forest University and the Eastman School of Music. His book, *Beethoven: The Ninth Symphony*, was re-published by Yale University Press in 2005. He was interviewed by Kerry Candaele and Kelly Candaele.

Could you describe the intellectual and political background to the Ninth?

The ideals of the Enlightenment meant a great deal to Beethoven. As the Enlightenment faded away and gave way to the new Romantic view of the world, Beethoven refused to give up certain cherished beliefs. And perhaps the finale of the Ninth was his last chance to give expression to those ideals.

What are the origins of the "Ode To Joy"?

Beethoven had shown an interest in Schiller's poem, *An die freude* (Ode to Joy) very early in his life. The poem itself was published in 1785, and Schiller wrote it as a kind of drinking song, to celebrate the rejoining of a circle of friends. Beethoven's interest in the poem started quite early, in the 1790s, when he was still a student in Bonn. And he had the intention of setting the whole poem to music.

But for some reason Beethoven didn't go ahead with that project in the 1790s, but the message of the poem and its expression of joy, as being a uniter, as expressing the feeling of good people enjoying each others company, appealed to Beethoven — and even in the politics of the poem, because the poem, in its original form, is quite political. One of the lines we know from the poem, *alle menschen warden bruder* (all men become brothers), was originally "beggars become the brothers of princes." Well, that's a pretty revolutionary idea. When you think about the date of the poem, 1785, you are in the foreshadow of the French Revolution.

So in some ways Schiller's poem is a precursor of revolutionary ideals. Well, Beethoven was actually circumspect about which parts of the poem he chose to set to music. He chose in all cases the less radical reading of the poem, and set only a small portion of the poem to music when he turned to the Ninth Symphony.

So the project had been in the back of his mind for a very long time. So why in the 1820s does he turn to Schiller again? Well maybe he felt this was his last chance to give expression to the sentiments of that poem. But he seized on essentially two messages. One, joy as the divine spark that unites people in universal brotherhood, and the idea of a loving deity who above all of this, keeping a loving shelter over humanity. He brought these two ideas together in the finale of the Ninth.

There are many who want to hear a Christian message in Beethoven's Ninth. How do you respond to these assertions?

When you think about autocratic regimes, of divine rights of kings, of an aristocracy, a ruling class and the masses of people being subordinate to that ruling class, you think of a kind of church, if you will, an orthodox church, where people bow down and pray to the ground. Beethoven wouldn't want people bowing down and praying to the ground; he would want them to pray with their hands open. If you look at *The Beethoven Frieze* by Gustav Klimt in Vienna, you'll see the heavenly chorus with their hands open and their eyes turned upwards, lifting oneself up, the dignity of the human being affirmed.

That's what Beethoven is telling us. Even the direction of the melody, the musical phrase, it rises up higher and higher and higher, almost physically lifting us up from the dust into something of worth and dignity. The idea of humanity lifting itself up from oppression is a very important theme in the Ninth Symphony. The question is asked in the poem, "do you want to discover your creator oh world?" So he's saying, if you are looking for God, if you are looking for that which makes the world happen, don't bow your head into the dust. Lift yourselves up and look to the canopy above us. Surely, Schiller and Beethoven say, a loving father must dwell there.

Now, some have read that loving father idea as the loving father that Beethoven never had in reality. His father was an alcoholic, abusive, a very rough man, and Beethoven never had any sentimental thoughts about him. So maybe, in a way, this became the surrogate father for him, but I think it's more than just a personal expression, and more of a universal expression of loving protective deity of some kind. Call it God if you will, but what makes the finale of the Ninth Symphony and the text that Beethoven used universally appealing, is that it is non-specific. That's one of the reasons why the

Ninth Symphony is universally loved.

After the first two performances in 1824, the Ninth almost disappeared from the Vienna repertory. Why?

There were no good orchestras to play it. Even for the 1824 performances, Beethoven had to bring together musicians from various existing ensembles in Vienna to make it happen, and then pay them out of his pocket. So it might be said that the Vienna Philharmonic came into existence solely for performing the Ninth Symphony well. By that time, the Ninth had become the kind of "sacred cow," the ceremonial piece *par excellence* that it still is.

But as time went on, the Ninth had its ups and downs in terms of its acceptance.

Yes, throughout the 19th century the Ninth Symphony was considered a controversial work. It took a while for it to settle in. It had to be performed many times, and be performed well, before audiences embraced it more universally.

There is a lot going in the music of the Ninth: joy, tragedy, melancholy, fear and a sweep of other emotions. How do you understand the piece as a whole?

There are views of life that understand it as a tragic thing? But do we live in despair? No, we overcome that despair with hope. We live with the possibility of hope always there, but with a certain realization that the world is a place filled with tragedy. But in the Ninth there is a sense of great exaltation, somehow as sense of tragedy being overcome.

Let's talk about the Fourth Movement.

The finale begins in chaos, with this "fanfare of horror" (*schreckensfanfare*) to use Wagner's term. But Beethoven then says "not these sounds" as the baritone soloist stands and sings the first words of the symphony: not these sounds of warfare, sounds of conflict, sounds of ugliness, but rather something more pleasant, more full of joy.

Beethoven says: "Here's the model. Are you up to the challenge? Are you up to this ideal?" Sometimes I think in my darkest despair that we fail, again, and again, and again. But we keep turning out for performances of the Ninth Symphony, don't we? We keep going back, regenerating hope, time and time again, and we take that journey, from silence through despair and tragedy, through farce, through serenity and the hymn-like nature of the third movement, to the optimism of the finale. We want to have that experience. Beethoven is giving us an idealistic expression of belief, that adversity can be overcome, that the human spirit can rise above our deepest and darkest impulses: our impulses toward warfare, toward cruelty, our impulses toward despair to one of optimism and hope.

But is it enough for us to experience this vicariously through Beethoven's music? I think the best performance of the Ninth Symphony, is the one where you come out the other end a better person. More willing to embrace those ideals, and to make the world a better place.

Barenboim, Beethoven and the Divan in New York

By Greg Mitchell
The Nation, February 5, 2013

Edward Said, the influential Palestinian-American writer and academic—and longtime *Nation* contributor—passed away nearly ten years ago, but his legacy lives on in many ways, including musically. With famed pianist and conductor Daniel Barenboim, he founded the West-Eastern Divan Orchestra in 1999, a unique assembly of mainly young Arab and Israeli musicians, a symbol for collaboration, peace and understanding now known around the world. They performed, in risky and unprecedented events, in Ramallah and in the demilitarized zone between North and South Korea, for example.

As I've often written: the two men deserve a Nobel Peace Prize, even if for Said it would be posthumous.

The Divan, with Barenboim conducting, performed all nine Beethoven symphonies at London's famed "Proms" concerts last summer, and now they have repeated the cycle at Carnegie Hall in New York. I attended the concluding program with the Second and Ninth symphonies, which was exciting, moving and at the close met with an ovation that went on seemingly forever. Said, a fine pianist in his own right, was passionate about Beethoven, and wrote about him in his final piece, for *The Nation*.

Last week, before beginning the cycle of symphonies, Barenboim brought several of the members of the orchestra to the hip Greenwich Village club, Le Poisson Rouge, for a very special event, dedicated to Said. Besides Barenboim's son, Michael, the names of the musicians alone tell a story: Nabih Bulos, Tyme Khleifi, Yael Rubinstein, Yamen Saadi, Maya Rasooly, Orhan Celibi, Hassan Moataz el Molla, Kinan Azmeh.

At the start, they welcomed Said's widow Mariam, who is now vice-president of Barenboim's organization in New York. Then clarinetist Azmeh, who hails from Damascus, played the eloquent "Prayer for Edward Said," solo. After a violin Boulez piece from Michael Barenboim, Azmeh returned with Daniel and Michael Barenboim to play a short extract from Bartók. They closed the program with all (except the senior Barenboim) playing Mendelssohn's famed Octet, op. 20—a stirring performance that drew a rapturous response. It was all the more powerful as the musicians from different, often hostile, countries traded lines or merged with incredible musical sympathy.

Then a host from the stage announced that there was an "after-party" — with a funky mix provided, of course, by another Barenboim son, David.

And the Barenboim-Said message will live on, permanently. From the program notes: "In November 2012, Maestro Barenboim announced the formation of the Barenboim-Said Academy in Berlin, Germany, which will upon its opening in 2015 translate the experience of the West-Eastern Divan Orchestra into a permanent, year-round institution for young musicians from the Middle East, building on the legacy of Edward W. Said's work. In addition to music instruction, students will receive a core curriculum in arts and humanities. Housed in a building adjacent to the Staatsoper, the Academy will feature a concert hall designed by renowned architect Frank Gehry."

BIBLIOGRAPHY

Books

Daniel Barenboim, *A Life in Music.*
Leonard Bernstein, *The Joy of Music.*
Jonathan Biss, *Beethoven's Shadow.*
Tim Blanning: *The Romantic Revolution..*
Tim Blanning, *The Triumph of Music.*
Charles Breunig, *The Age of Revolution and Reaction,1789-1848*
Michael Broyles, *Beethoven in America.*
Esteban Buch, *Beethoven's Ninth: A Political History.*
Scott G. Burnham, *Beethoven Hero.*
Barry Cooper: *Beethoven.*
Tia DeNora, *Beethoven and The Construction of Genius.*
Rita Dove, *Sonata Mulattica.*

Michael Hamburger, *Beethoven's Letters, Journals, and Conversations.*

Eric Hobsbawm, *The Age of Revolution.*

H.E. Krehbiel, How to Listen to Music.

David Benjamin Levy, *Beethoven: The Ninth Symphony.*

Lawrence Kramer, *Why Classical Music Still Matters.*

Basil Lam, *Beethoven String Quartets.*

H.C. Robbins Landon, *Beethoven.*

Lewis Lockwood, Beethoven: *The Music and the Life.*

Russell Martin, *Beethoven's Hair.*

Edmund Morris, *Beethoven: The Universal Composer*

Alex Ross, *The Rest Is Noise.*

Harvey Sachs, *The Ninth: Beethoven And The World In 1824.*

Oliver Sacks, *Musicophilia.*

Edward Said, *On Late Style.*

Maynard Soloman, *Beethoven.*

Maynard Soloman, *Late Beethoven.*

Oscar Sonneck, *Beethoven: Impressions by his Contemporaries.*

J.W.N. Sullivan, *Beethoven: His Spiritual Development.*

Conrad Wilson, *Beethoven: 20 Critical Works.*

ACKNOWLEDGMENTS

Kerry Candaele wants to thank Chris Bottoms and Nick Higgins, whose skills with the camera and dedication to their art are unmatched. Thank you to Isabel Lipthay and Martin Firgau who introduced me to beautiful Chile, to Akira Taguachi, my guide through Japan, to Billy Bragg who welcomed me to England and showed the way, and to Feng Congde who still fights the good fight for a better China. A special thanks to the Los Angeles Daiku Singers and Yasu Tanano who took me to Naruto, Japan. And for support from the outset, thanks to Kevin McGrath, Nick Taylor, Hideki Obayashi, Kelly Candaele, Courtney Messenbaugh, Oliver Herder, Molly Wryn, Greg Miller, and to all of the Kickstarter comrades who weighed in with inspiration and kindness.

Greg Mitchell thanks Barbara Bedway for tips, items, links, running commentary on dozens of CDs and music downloads and concerts, and then a close edit on the final manuscript that resulted. Also thanks to Jeremy Denk and Joe Alessi, Susan Mitchell and Peter Herzfeld, Arlene Keiser, Ed Chang, and to Tim Page for helping to get me going with some inspiring Beethoven discussions.

ABOUT THE AUTHORS

Kerry Candaele has produced and directed several previous documentaries, including *Wal-Mart: The High Cost of Low Price*, and *Iraq For Sale* for Brave New Films, and co-produced *A League of Their Own*, the basis for the Tom Hanks film of that name. Candaele is the author of two books on United States history, and was the Richard Hofstadter Fellow in U.S. history at Columbia University. He has also written and produced CDs of his own music. He lives in Venice, California.

Greg Mitchell has authored more than a dozen books and currently writes on media and politics for *The Nation*. His books include *The Campaign of the Century: Upton Sinclair's Race for Governor of California and the Birth of Media Politics*, winner of the Goldsmith Book Prize; *Tricky Dick and the Pink Lady* (a New York Times Notable Book); *Atomic Cover-up* and with Robert Jay Lifton, *Hiroshima in America*. Mitchell was the editor of *Editor & Publisher* from 2002 to 2009. He lives in Nyack, N.Y.